WHY PEOPLE BUY

WHY PEOPLE BUY

John O'Shaughnessy

New York   Oxford • OXFORD UNIVERSITY PRESS

Oxford University Press

Oxford   New York   Toronto
Delhi   Bombay   Calcutta   Madras   Karachi
Petaling Jaya   Singapore   Hong Kong   Tokyo
Nairobi   Dar es Salaam   Cape Town
Melbourne   Auckland

and associated companies in
Berlin   Ibadan

First published in 1987 by Oxford University Press, Inc.
200 Madison Avenue, New York, New York 10016

First issued as an Oxford Unviersity Press paperback, 1989

Oxford is a registered trademark of Oxford University Press

Library of Congress Cataloging-in-Publication Data

O'Shaughnessy, John.
  Why people buy.

  Bibliography: p.
  Includes index.
  1. Consumers.   2. Motivation research (Marketing)
3. Purchasing.   I. Title.
HF5415.3.O84   1987   658.8'342   86-12511
ISBN 0-19-504086-4 (alk. paper)
ISBN 0-19-504087-2 (PBK)

10 9 8 7 6 5 4 3 2

Printed in the United States of America

Preface

This book attempts to capture some of the richness of the reasons why people buy. It is organized and written in a way that should be useful to practitioners in marketing. It should also be a valuable supplement in courses on consumer behavior.

Not surprisingly most of the research on consumer behavior to date has drawn on mainstream psychology for its inspiration and methods. However, the results have not had the impact anticipated on marketing management in spite of the belief among those in marketing that an understanding of consumer psychology is basic to consumer marketing.

This book does draw partially on the current literature and research on consumer behavior but it is more concerned with promoting an approach that is all but ignored at present. This is the interpretive social science approach. As applied in this book it simply means we record what consumers say before they buy, during buying, and after buying and seek to *interpret* such "protocol statements" to discover the reasons and rules guiding brand choice. Over the past twelve years my students and I have collected more than a thousand such protocols covering all types of products. This book stems from an attempt at interpreting these protocols to discover insights and generalities about buying behavior in respect to brand choice. However, interpretation is never done in a vacuum but is always guided to some extent by prior ideas as to what might be found. Although some of these prior ideas were drawn from the literature on consumer behavior, the main ideas and organizing concepts came from a branch of mental philosophy known as "the theory of action." Philosophers examine the logical properties and core meanings and usage of words like want, decision, choice, intention, preference, and the like. In conceptually distinguishing these terms, philosophers have in the process developed insights, classifications, and schemata that provide clear notions for studying intentional actions like buying.

Whatever the merits of the book, it would be much poorer but for the unstinting help I received from colleagues and others. Roger Dickinson, Ann Beattie, Luis Garcia, Robert Lear, N. J. O'Shaughnessy, Alfred Oxenfeldt, Joel Steckel, Debra Stephens, Wilfried Vanhonacker, and Charles Wiseman provided criticism on an early version of the manuscript that proved invaluable in developing the final draft. Don Lehmann gave me valuable advice on subsequent drafts, while Morris Holbrook's comments led me to rewrite a number of sections. My research assistant Bob Stinerock paid close attention to the text to catch any logical slips, ambiguities, and vagueness. Finally, I would like to thank the many students who collected the protocols over the years, some of which are included in this book: the long but very useful one in Chapter 6 was written by Stephen Bell, a current Ph.D. candidate, who also helped in other ways. I am very grateful to them all but would remind the reader that I alone am responsible for the views expressed and the errors that remain.

Many examples from business history are used to illustrate an argument and enliven the text. Some of the best of these came from those two delightful books *Top Sellers USA* by Molly Wade McGrath and *Advertising the American Dream* by Roland Marchand.

December 1986   John O'Shaughnessy
New York City

Contents

WHY PEOPLE BUY

Introduction:
An Overview

The purpose of this book is to equip those in consumer market-ing with the knowledge and tools needed to bring marketing strategy in line with consumers' motivations. The knowledge portion of the book consists mainly of descriptions of consumer behavior in different states of readiness to buy. To focus the knowledge we gain of consumers, we will use a tool I call the *consumer protocol statement.* The protocol statement as used in this book is a record of consumers "thinking aloud" before they buy (anticipatory accounts), during buying (contemporaneous accounts), and after buying (retrospective accounts). We analyze such protocol statements using knowledge gained in the text to identify consumers' goals, wants, beliefs, and choice criteria, and how such information might be used in market planning. The protocol statements are real cases selected by the author from well over a thousand of them collected by the author or his students.

Figure 1 shows the view of the consumer that is basic to the structure of the book. Consumers are seen as having goals, wants, and beliefs that dispose them to buy. However, consum-ers may be disposed toward buying a product without actually doing so. In Figure 1, this is labeled "Wanting without buying." The category next to it is "Buying without deciding." Here, the consumer is ready to buy without feeling the need for delibera-tion. The final category, "Deciding before buying," describes those buying situations in which the buyer feels the need to deliberate about what to buy. We will briefly review the contri-bution each chapter makes to the overall purpose of the book.

Chapter 1 discusses the role of the consumer's goals, wants,

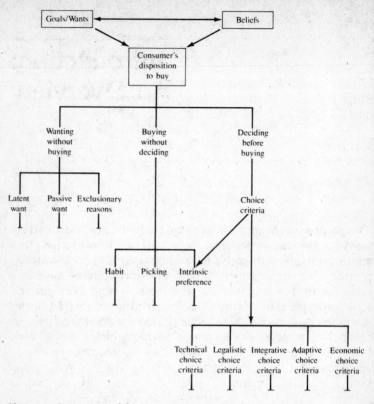

Figure 1   Basic View of the Consumer

and beliefs. We begin with the premise that all people have a vision of the good life that manifests itself in a set of goals toward which consumers consciously or subconsciously strive. Such goals find part of their expression in a demand for products that contribute to the good life or the preferred life vision. However, since consumers' visions of the good life are apt to be hazy, it is possible to influence their goals.

Marketing can and does influence the adoption of goals by helping consumers visualize what it would be like—("what it *really* would be like")—to achieve the state of affairs described by the goal. Similarly, marketing can influence goal priorities by dramatizing the consequences of neglecting a particular goal (e.g., the goal of good health). When consumers seek a goal such as good health, there are an infinite number of ways of going about achieving it, such as taking vitamins, having regular checkups, exercising regularly, and so on. This means that goals do not precisely determine product wants. However, a consumer's bundle of wants is not a random collection but a coordinated system of wants that represents a specification of the good life. For consumers to want a certain product they must believe that the product plays a role in achieving the good life and that the product coheres with lifestyle, values, and belief systems.

Chapter 2 considers the fact that consumers want many products without meaning to buy them. Knowing why this is so helps us to better understand buying:

- Consumers may want a product but their want for it may remain "latent" because they are not aware of what the product can do for them. Consumers can thus be aware of the existence of a product without realizing the potential of that product for meeting their goals.
- Consumers may be aware of the potential benefits of a product but be inhibited from buying. In such a situation, the want is described as "passive."
- Consumers may be held back from buying by "exclusionary" reasons that take them, temporarily or permanently, out of the market (e.g., shortage of money, promises to others, and so on).

In calculating market potential, marketing managers need to take account of the extent to which they can activate latent and passive wants to increase market penetration and the extent to which market penetration is dampened by exclusionary factors.

Chapter 3 develops the theory that buying behavior follows certain rules. If consumers simply behaved at random, there would be no discernible rationality in what they did, so understanding their behavior would be impossible. However, if consumers act "as if" following rules—rules that make sense—it might be possible to identify such rules and design a marketing strategy to fit them. Understanding the behavior of others rests on the assumption of shared interpretations of the rules being followed. Chapter 3 argues that the rules used by consumers can be extracted from anticipatory, contemporaneous, and retrospective protocol statements by focusing on the key words or constructs used by customers. Thus, if someone says a particular brand was purchased because it was the most familiar, it is the word "familiarity" that reveals the rule being followed—"Other things being equal, I buy the brand that is most familiar."

Chapter 4 assumes that some brand choices are not the result of any meaningful decision. This theory runs counter to the claim that all brand choices are the output of a decision. Such a claim, however, uses the term "decision" loosely. In this book, "decision" is reserved for situations that are sufficiently problematic for the consumer to feel the need to deliberate priorities and evaluate the likely costs and benefits attached to rival offerings. Where the consumer considers a simple buying situation, there is no perceived practical uncertainty and no need for a decision.

Just as the consumer usually chooses rather than decides to eat breakfast, so the consumer does not always decide each time what product or brand to buy. In the case of habit, the consumer follows a rule to buy in accordance with past buying practice. This chapter considers how habits might be broken or reinforced. In the case of "picking," the consumer follows the rule of randomly picking from among a cluster of brands in the belief that whatever differences exist among the brands, they are irrelevant for his or her purposes. In the case of "intrinsic preference," brand choice is based purely on subjective liking—consumers buy what they like the most. Consumers who are asked why they chose the brand they did only talk about the type of enjoyment they anticipated (e.g., an exciting show, a smooth whiskey, a strong fragrance, and so on). This chapter discusses how intrinsic preferences can be reinforced or changed by exposing the consumer to additional choice criteria.

Chapter 5 considers the degree of rationality in buying. Consumers often get the facts wrong about a product or brand. This may be due to bias arising from a wish to believe something were true. Even when consumers do get the facts right, they may err in the way they process information because of either wishful thinking or poor reasoning. In pointing out these areas of bias and error, Chapter 5 stresses the importance of taking such behavior into account in market planning.

Chapters 6 and 7 are concerned with identifying and discussing the objective considerations (i.e., the choice criteria) that enter into consumer decision-making. Whenever choice is based on objective reasons, it reflects "extrinsic preference." Extrinsic preference is the opposite of intrinsic preference, which is a matter of subjective feeling and reaction. Products are bought to perform certain functions or to produce certain effects. The choice criteria used by consumers to evaluate rival brands stem from wanting to achieve these functions or effects. Excluding intrinsic preference, the choice criteria fall into one or more of the following categories.

- **Technical criteria** These criteria embrace the physical attributes and performance characteristics that are sought by the consumer.
- **Legalistic criteria** These criteria are imposed or emanate from outside agencies (e.g., government insistence on wearing seat belts in cars).
- **Integrative criteria** These criteria reflect the consumer's concern with being better integrated with self or with community.
- **Adaptive criteria** These criteria refer to the adaptations that occur in coming to terms with information overload and decision uncertainty.
- **Economic criteria** These criteria are used to rank alternatives on the basis of the relative sacrifice being demanded.

Finally, Chapter 8 discusses those aspects of the decision-making process that help to pull the book together while at the same time explaining such concepts as "preference," "intention," and "satisfaction." A good deal of marketing research is concerned with determining preferences, predicting choices from buying intentions, and judging marketing success in terms of buyer satisfaction. Each of these purposes assumes a clear definition of these terms when in fact, considerable conceptual confusion arises from their use.

This brief overview has focused on those aspects of consumer behavior that are elaborated on in the text. For many readers, however, the major interest lies in application: How should marketing managers apply what is relevant to their own market situation? The first step is the collection of protocol statements. The next step is to analyze these protocols to determine their implications for marketing strategy. Such analyses are illustrated in the text (see Chapters 6 and 7). A careful reading of the protocols and the analyses is essential reading if applications are to be understood.

In stressing the analyses of protocol statements, the book is implicitly telling managers to "listen" to the consumer. If we wish to know what consumers want, believe, and think, there is no adequate substitute for the consumer's own testimony. However, how we go about listening, recording, and analyzing the testimony will depend on our purposes and the "theories" we hold as to what is relevant to our marketing problems.

This book assumes that the marketing manager is intent on improving the firm's marketing strategy to achieve a better fit with the wants and beliefs of the consumer. The description of buyer behavior forms the basis for interpreting the testimony of consumers as recorded in the protocol statements. However, the analyses of protocol statements also provide a rich background for interpreting the usual market survey data. The marketing manager should understand the diversity of beliefs and wants in a market—including the recognition that consumers may choose the same thing for very different reasons. The final choice of brand can be the culmination of a whole series of choices based on a wide range of choice criteria. Marketing management needs to take account of such choice criteria in devising a marketing strategy.

1

Consumer Goals, Wants, and Beliefs

This book seeks to explain why people (1) buy at all and (2) why they buy the products and brands they do. If the question why people buy at all seems somewhat rhetorical, it is only because we seldom look beyond accepting buying as a matter of necessity. But to claim we buy as a matter of necessity does scant justice to the variety of purchases made and the motives at work. We will look first at the complexity of buying goals.

CONSUMER GOALS

Buying is a purposive activity, motivated and directed by the belief that the consequences of buying make life that much happier. But there is little guidance as to how happiness might be achieved—and certainly no guidance to consumers on what they should buy to achieve it. Consumer buying, however, tracks certain life goals that reflect a vision of the good life. People are sensitive to contrasts in the human condition; therefore, they prefer to be

- Healthy *not* ill.
- Full of life *not* miserable and sluggish.
- Physically secure *not* physically threatened.
- Loved and admired *not* hated and shunned.
- Insiders *not* outsiders looking in.
- Confident *not* insecure.
- Serene/relaxed *not* tense and anxious.
- Beautiful *not* ugly.
- Rich *not* poor.
- Clean *not* dirty.
- Knowledgeable *not* ignorant.
- In control of life *not* at the mercy of events.
- Entertained *not* bored.

The agreeable polar extremes represent the life goals or the preferred life vision. Leymore (1975) argues that consumer advertising should strongly link its appeals to such goals on the ground that effective advertising must always offer—however obliquely—the possibility of enhancing the target audience's chances of achieving life goals. Advertising acknowledges this by showing how the product enhances the "good life." It is one reason that advertising focuses on consumer experiences and satisfactions with the product rather than on the product itself.

Since multiple life goals constitute the preferred life vision, the consumer must order them, subordinating one to the other, so that at any one time the consumer has preferences for one life goal over another (e.g., beauty over additional knowledge). This ordering of goals is a manifestation of the consumer's value system, which is another way of saying consumers' goals are determined by some basic structure of preferences. Different value systems result in different lifestyles. But the adoption of any one lifestyle imposes a loss to the consumer that the rejected way of life would have provided. Hence, the consumer is often indecisive as to which value system to adopt.

When people cannot make up their minds about goals it is not because they do not know what they want—they want full attainment of all the goals constituting the preferred life vision—but because they are still deciding priorities. Sometimes one goal may be manifestly subordinate to another, such as when the goal of being healthy is given priority over more social involvement. However, according to Nozick (1981), a sufficient number of lower level goals may collectively receive priority. For example, long-term health may be sacrificed to achieve the numerous instant gratifications with which it conflicts.

Value systems are largely culturally determined. Social living itself suggests what problems are key and what conduct generates social approval. Mary Douglas (1979), an anthropologist, claims that beyond bare needs, the key goals in buying are indeed social. These social goals (see Figure 2) are meant to:

- Signal to others the consumer's rank, values, and preferred self-image.

Many products, for example house furnishings and clothes, are highly visible and regarded as indicative of the owner's values. Such visible purchases are intended to communicate a

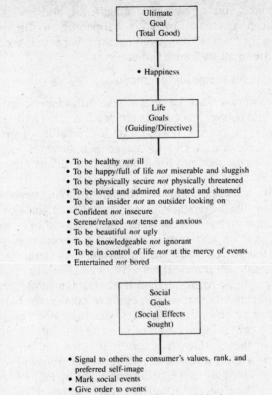

Figure 2   Consumer Goals

favorable image. They cater to such life goals as wanting to be admired, beautiful, socially accepted, and so on.

● Mark social occasions that are thought worthy of reaffirmation.

In every culture there are occasions (e.g., birth and marriages) to be marked or recognized with special purchases such as christening robes, graduation gowns, wedding dresses, tuxedos, and so on.

● Give order to events so as to make sense of the world around.

Some products like newspapers, magazines, and books are bought to keep abreast of what is happening in the world around. Even the "novel" was given its name because it brought news about life in all its forms and contrasts.

● Increase time for social involvement.

✗ Vacuum cleaners, washing machines, dishwashers, microwave ovens, and convenience foods are products that reduce the need for regular chores and release time for social involvement and private activities. A rise in the general level of income always increases the demand for products that reduce the regularity of chores.

Although we have spoken of the consumer having goals, this does not mean that buyers are fully aware of such goals or are able to describe with transparent clarity the relationship between their buying actions and some set of goals. Consumers may overlook or fail to recognize the importance of certain goals which they might well pursue if helped to visualize what attaining the goals might do to enrich their lives (Putnam, 1981). Educational establishments that entice people to take on the burden of getting a degree or continuing their education, for example, tempt them by providing a vision of what additional education would mean to their futures. The aim is to alter goal priorities by dramatizing what it would *really* be like to reemphasize some neglected goal. Thus, one advertising campaign by Pan Am centered on reminding people about the importance of knowing their roots by vacationing in the land of their forebears.

Goals may be given renewed attention by consumers if the advertised solution can be shown to be realizable (not utopian), recognizable, and socially approved progress toward the goal. For instance, in recent years consumers have come to believe that (1) good health and fitness are realizable goals that are somewhat within their control (through diet and exercise), (2) progress is recognizable (e.g., lowered cholesterol level), and (3) society reinforces the pursuit of such goals. Hence, renewed attention has been given to personal fitness.

It is important to recognize that consumers can and do question their own values. In some cases, their soul-searching can lead to a transformation of what they want out of life (Dilman, 1981). Because people often feel they lack sources of advice on how to live life at its best, advertising has been able to fill the void by "showing" how others get more out of life (Marchand, 1985).

CONSUMER WANTS

Goals Underdetermine Wants

Having goals implies a *disposition* to seek the state of affairs described by the goals. But the description typically *underdetermines* (i.e., does not completely determine) what activities should be undertaken or which products should be sought to achieve the goals. There is no one-to-one relationship between goals and wants—goals are much too general for this purpose. Thus, the description of good health refers to freedom from bodily ailments and feeling fit, but not to the innumerable activities and products relating to this purpose.

In any case, an individual purchase generally is part of some overall consumption system or lifestyle, rather than an isolated event. The problem for the consumer is not identifying expressions of the preferred life vision, but determining an overall lifestyle or consumption pattern that represents an acceptable specification of goals. Consumer wants form a coordinated system that is shaped by what the consumer believes to be a desirable and feasible way of life that reflects the preferred life vision. However, when consumers are motivated by only a general sense of goals and have a flexible value system, they are open to persuasion as to what products to buy.

Nature of Wants

To *want* a particular product is to have a disposition toward using, consuming, or possessing that product. Wants are always identified in terms of a disposition to some action. Thus, if someone wants a car he or she is a "suspect" for buying a car since having the want means a disposition toward possessing the car. This, in turn, suggests the possibility of future buying. Wants express goals since goals subsume wants. Wants express goals in the sense that we can see the preferred life vision in the want itself without the inference process that would be needed if wants were simply means to goal attainment (Taylor, 1979). A person's collective wants are a disposition toward a certain lifestyle and the preferred life vision. If consumers are free to choose, they will choose only that which is wanted (or likely to be wanted)—which leads to the marketing truism that wanting something is a necessary condition for buying something and not wanting something is a sufficient condition for not buying it.

Once we accept that the preferred life vision or even a lifestyle finds expression in many equally acceptable ways, it follows that many wants are often substitutable without any sense of corresponding loss. Persuasion can lead to the substitution of one want for another want when both reflect the same goal, just as TV substitutes to some extent for the movies. Even where a want has crystallized into wanting a specific product class, the want can still remain vague on specifics until the time for purchase. Consumers, in fact, often know what they do not want but otherwise remain open to persuasion.

Desires and some needs are special types of wants. A "desire" is a want which an individual is acutely aware of not having realized, while a "need" is a want that is a basic requirement or a universal want such as the need for food. Most wants are neither desires nor needs but just plain wants, like the want for a toothpaste. Most wants are not like hunger pangs compelling satisfaction but are simply the inclinations that are weighed in the choice process.

The concept of a want carries with it a number of implications:

- The consumer is not always conscious of his or her wants until some stimulus, like advertising, facilitates recall or activates the want.

- The consumer may buy a product in anticipation of wanting it, so that reminding the consumer to plan for the future may help generate current sales.

- Consumers may want something they do not need (e.g., cigarettes) but they can also need something they do not want since a need that is not being met (e.g., job skills for the unemployed) may not always manifest itself in a want to remedy the deficiency.

- *Active* wants weight the feasibility of satisfying a want, so that expressed wants do not necessarily take into account all secret wants. A consumer may rule out wants for products that are beyond his or her budget or wants for products that are not available. But wants that are currently nonrealizable may remain active and prompt action to remedy the position (e.g., saving for a down payment on a house). In any case, it is important for the seller to facilitate the attainment of wants (e.g., through the provision of credit).

- An individual consumer's want can be described as a "cluster concept," that is, a want can be thought of as a cluster of attributes not all of which must be possessed by an offering for the consumer to feel the want is being met. Thus there are several makes of car that a particular consumer believes will meet his want because they all display the crucial performances that are sought. However, no single car displays all the exact attributes the individual consumer wants.

- Consumers may actually want something they do not consciously believe they want. Conversely, consumers may think they want what in fact they do not want. Wanting something is neither a necessary nor sufficient condition for the consumer to be satisfied with the product after it is bought. What consumers might want with *perfect* understanding of their goals may differ widely from what is currently wanted. A husband and wife may believe they want an apartment in the city, but when they reflect on their true goals of a quiet, relaxed lifestyle, they find a house in the country would better meet their needs.

Goal priorities and product wants change as the lifestyles of consumers change. Some wants just *disappear*. For example, the change in lifestyle radically reduced the demand for men's hats. Old wants are *replaced* by new wants when new products come along that perform better. Entirely *new* wants also arise. An increase in income, for example, makes realizable what may previously have been considered a pipe dream (e.g., possession of a sports car). This also leads to a demand for a better match between what is wanted and what is offered. This, in turn, leads to increasing market segmentation as manufacturers seek to cater to different sets of more refined wants. In every market, from toothpaste to washing machines, the trend toward increasing segmentation has been unremitting.

Entirely new wants can arise as a result of persuading the consumer that a product is a novel expression of goals. Take, for example, deodorants. Until recent times the elimination of body odor was not believed to be an expression of any life goal;

body odor was unselfconsciously accepted. But the absence of body odor became an important subgoal when in the last century certain groups associated body odor with dangers to health. The suggestion was made that, like the foul smell of open sewers and stagnant waters, inhaling body odor was injurious to health. But more important was the later association made between body odor and lack of cleanliness, the lower classes, animals, and sexual promiscuity. In 1933, an advertising magazine proposed a 21-gun salute to an advertising agency for scaring so many consumers into doing something about their B.O. (Marchand, 1985)!

A basic question is whether advertising can create new product wants without these wants expressing goals. Certainly, consumers do buy products which they were not actively seeking before being made aware of them. Some of these new products may simply be better solutions to old problems, in which case no new want is created. However, some new products perform a function not previously regarded as a problem until the new product solved it! Thus we have the recent spate of "skin repair" products claiming to help speed the natural repair of damaged skin cells. While most consumers may not have been aware of the possibility of damaged skin cells, it cannot be denied that such products are purporting to meet the universal goals of health and beauty. In other words, the want for the product was latent until activiated by the consumer being made aware of the product's function.

People are not always conscious of what they might want. Someone who is not conscious of being cold will not actively try to keep warm. On being told he looks cold, however, the person might reply "Now that you mention it, I am. . . . ." The want is realized. And so it is with other so-called created wants. Consumers will not knowingly go against their own perceived self-interests even though they are not necessarily able to spell out precisely what those self-interests are.

What seems to be meant, however, by "creating wants" is not that firms are capable of creating a demand for products that serve no purpose, but that many wants are "artificial." This is an old debate. In the first century A.D., Seneca attributed the evils of civilization to the stimulation of artificial wants. This charge was resurrected in the nineteenth century by socialists claiming that all the evils of society were due to the inculcation of artificial needs. However, any distinction between artificial and natural wants is necessarily arbitrary and simply reflects differences in values. Taking the argument to extremes, only the bare necessities of life can be defended as nonartificial while everything else, including the whole of culture with a capital C, can be regarded as artificial.

CONSUMER BELIEFS

Nature of Beliefs

A "want" has content when it is thought of as an anticipated benefit. When the want becomes want of a specific product, the consumer has a *belief* that the product can provide some, most, or all of the anticipated benefits.

A *belief* is a disposition to accept that certain statements are more likely to be true than false (or vice versa) or that certain things should be done (or not done). *Beliefs are the principal guides to what actions should be taken to satisfy wants.* Advertising therefore tries to link its appeals to generally held beliefs. Many advertisements for deodorants, for example, exploit the commonly held belief that others are likely to reject us on the most trivial of grounds so that "image management" rather than real worth is what counts.

Perception and Belief

Sometimes the term *perception* is used as a synonym for belief. But the term perception can be used in a number of different senses:

- As the *faculty* of appreciating the world especially through the senses.
- As the *process* of receiving, interpreting, or organizing sensory inputs.
- As the *product* or result which is the consequence of receiving, interpreting, or organizing sensory input.

It is perception as a product that is used as a synonym for belief since underlying all perceptions is a set of implicit beliefs. People commonly substitute perception for belief when they wish to avoid the suggestion that beliefs are necessarily conscious beliefs. Thus, saying the consumer *perceives* no difference between two rival brands carries fewer overtones of conscious prior awareness than saying the consumer *believes* there is no difference between the two brands.

Beliefs and Action

Beliefs control and inform intentional action all the way from shaping wants into specific product preferences to guiding post-purchase actions, such as returning an unsatisfactory product. A consumer may believe he or she has a certain want. But even if that want amounts to a strong desire, it does not follow that the consumer will rush out and act on the want. Beliefs as to the consequences of acting on the want immediately come to mind—including beliefs about the relationship between the consequences of buying in relation to what is wanted and beliefs about the consequences of buying in relation to the satisfaction or frustration of other wants.

Consumer beliefs about products possess content in terms of what product attributes (e.g., furniture covers made of plastic) produce what effects (e.g., looking cheap). It is beliefs about the effect of a product having or not having a certain feature (e.g., a diesel engine) at a certain level (e.g., size of engine) that primarily determines the consumer's choice criteria. In addition, beliefs about what is or might be available at what prices also influence choice criteria by helping to ensure such choice criteria can be realistically met.

Relatively few beliefs may guide and constrain the consumer when a purchase is first contemplated. Acquiring additional beliefs through information is one way consumers can narrow the search for what they want. On occasion, though, initial beliefs can determine purchase. A purchase may, for example, be prompted by an advertisement if the advertised product (e.g., a dress) is believed to be the best one to buy. Initial beliefs may also direct shopping strategy. As one woman put it: "Everyone thinks I am lucky to have a whole apartment to furnish from scratch. But it is, in fact, a rather anxious time with no room for mistakes and no chance of extravagances. So I will need to shop around to make sure I will have no regrets."

Initial beliefs can range from general ideas about what is wanted to highly specific beliefs about a product class (e.g., "I wanted a wool carpet since past experience shows that wool is the only material that wears really well") to specific beliefs about brands (e.g., "Sony is a good name"). This happens because consumers start the buying process with different levels of experience.

Conscious Versus Latent Beliefs

We have spoken of beliefs "coming to mind" as if only conscious beliefs influence behavior. This is not so. Implicit in every act of buying are beliefs we take for granted. Some may never have been thought about, even though they would be readily endorsed if they were examined. Such beliefs are called *latent beliefs*. For example, consumers in the United States implicitly assume that stores will not be out of stock. Where experience shows such assumptions to be untrue, buying patterns change radically.

There are other beliefs that might not be openly endorsed if exposed. Such beliefs may reflect on the consumer's self-image or they may be socially imprudent. Thus, even at the trivial level, few consumers come right out and say they bought something because they believed it signals their good taste—and affluence—to the world. But the reasons for these purchases are often implied when people talk about them.

Evidence and Belief Certainty

Beliefs are held with different degrees of certainty, but seldom (if ever) with complete certitude. As a consequence, beliefs about products and brands are seldom incorrigible and immutable but are open to correction and change through learning. As Adler (1985) points out, we sometimes "use the word 'belief' to signify that we have some measure of doubt about the opinion we claim to be true. . . ." When truths are necessary truths (e.g., parallel lines never meet), they are not prefaced by the word "belief."

If beliefs are, for all practical purposes, neither incorrigible nor immutable and *beliefs enter into buying*, then new information via an advertising campaign always holds out the possibility of changing buyer behavior. This is a statement of the obvious, yet it seems to conflict with the finding that an advertisement need not necessarily be believed to be effective. This can be misleading unless it is appreciated that the opposite of belief is not disbelief but *doubt*. A consumer may doubt the claims of an advertisement and still buy the product as a result of seeing the advertisement because

- The disputed claims are irrelevant to the consumer's want and the product's other attributes elicit purchase.
- A less exaggerated form of the claim—enough to stimulate purchase—is believed.
- The purchase involves little risk or potential regret and the consumer believes he or she should give the product a try.

Few consumers buy a product on the basis of advertising they completely disbelieve. If it seems otherwise, it is likely that consumers doubt, rather than completely disbelieve the claims. This leads to a consideration of the evidential support consumers have for their beliefs.

It is expected that consumer certitude in respect to their beliefs is directly related to the supporting evidence. The relationship, however, is by no means perfect. Consumers harbor and cherish many beliefs about products and brands for which they could produce little evidence either from personal experience or elsewhere. When acquiring information is costly in time and effort, buying decisions may be based on impression. One purpose of advertising is to reduce the cost and effort of acquiring information, though the information provided by advertising may not be objectively balanced. In any case, consumer beliefs can be formed, changed, or reinforced by persuasion.

Wants and beliefs interact since wanting something to be true can influence the selection of those facts that reinforce existing presuppositions. We speak of a person having a bee in his bonnet or burying his head in the sand to indicate the persistence of preferred but erroneous beliefs. But consumers can also be blind to the truth because they so want to believe that there is a cure for cancer, a way of restoring youth, or a way to lose 25 pounds painlessly and in only two weeks.

GOALS, WANTS, AND BELIEFS

The relationship between beliefs, goals or wants, and buying actions is shown in Figure 3. Buying actions cohere and harmonize with the goals and wants of the consumer. They are undertaken only as long as the consumer believes the purchases are in line with his or her wants. But consumer goals and wants are circumscribed by beliefs about what is and is not feasible in

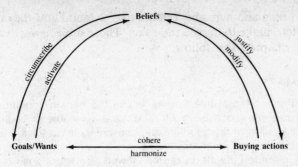

Figure 3 Model of Rationality *(Inspired by Laudan's [1984] Reticulated Model of Rationality)*

the context. However, goals and wants activate beliefs to determine goal and want priorities. Buying actions both depend on and influence beliefs since buying is justified by antecedent beliefs that are modified by the buying actions taken.

Reasons for contemplating buying can always be expressed in terms of wants and beliefs: consumer purchases are always perceived as articulations of wants and applications of beliefs. Reasons favoring buying can lead to an actual intention to buy. The mental process leading from wants and beliefs to buying intention is a form of practical reasoning along the lines first suggested by Aristotle and developed more recently by Anscombe (1972) and Von Wright (1983). The following is an illustration of the simplest level of practical reasoning:

Goals: To be knowledgeable not ignorant and to make sense of the world around.

1st premise: I want to keep abreast with the news.
2nd premise: Unless I buy and read a newspaper I will not be able to keep abreast of the news.
Conclusion: Therefore, I must buy and read a newspaper.

The goal expresses a vision of being knowledgeable rather than ignorant. The first premise expresses a "want." The second premise expresses a belief about a causal relationship. The conclusion prescribes the action to be taken. The "want" provides the motive, the "beliefs" steer the buying action taken.

However, the above illustration offers little insight into the buying decision process. We are interested in knowing how consumers weigh the pros and cons of buying one product or brand rather than another; what criteria they use; and how they resolve conflicts, make tradeoffs, and so on. These subjects are discussed in the chapters that follow.

SUMMARY

Consumers are sensitive to contrasts in the human condition (e.g., being healthy versus being ill). The more agreeable polar positions reflect a vision of the good life and consumers try to track this vision in their pattern of purchases.

The preferred life vision can be viewed as a set of goals to which consumers strive. All of these goals cannot be sought with equal vigor, so priorities are established in accordance with the consumer's value system. This value system tends to give priority to certain social goals concerned with building social bridges or erecting social fences. Value systems do not necessarily determine precisely how goals should be ranked. This means that goal priorities often are changed by dramatizing the favorable consequences of changing goal priorities.

To *want* a particular product is to have a disposition toward using, consuming, or possessing that product. Higher level goals typically underdetermine wants in that innumerable activities and products may be regarded as expressions of the same goal. Nonetheless, the product wants of a consumer form a coordinated system that is shaped by what the consumer believes to be an acceptable expression of the preferred life vision.

Within the constraints set by income and product availability, consumer *beliefs* about (1) the anticipated effects on satisfaction arising from possessing, consuming, or using the product and (2) what is available at what prices are the principal determinants of what is bought. Advertising and other forms of promotion can mold, change, or affect the certitude with which beliefs are held—thus affecting how wholeheartedly the consumer enters into buying the product.

IMPLICATIONS FOR MARKETING

1. To help achieve advertising impact, every consumer advertisement should be linked, however obliquely, to a vision of the good life and, where appropriate, should show the brand as facilitating social involvement.

2. To increase primary demand for a product, a firm should consider trying to change the relative importance the consumer attaches to the component of the good life relating to the product. This can be done by

   • Dramatizing the favorable consequences of changing priorities as to what constitutes the good life.

- Showing that such a change is realizable by using the firm's product.
- Showing increased satisfaction that is both recognizable and socially approved.

3. In new product development, the firm, should, where feasible, seek a novel expression of the good life. Newness always has its own appeal.

4. If a firm's offering is to be quickly accepted, it must be designed to fit the consumer's lifestyle. In addition, it must be coordinated with the consumption system of which the firm's offering is to be part.

5. What consumers say they want in terms of product attributes, and so forth, always reflects what is currently being offered and what it appears reasonable to want. A new product (e.g., a word processor) that offers a new way of meeting the basic functions or performance sought (e.g., in terms of typing) can lead to a radical revision of the product attributes consumers want.

6. If the firm is finding less customer satisfaction with its offering, competitive new promotions should be reviewed. The level of customer satisfaction is related to perceptions of the alternatives.

7. If a firm finds a steadily declining market, it should check for changes in lifestyle (e.g., more working mothers) that might make the decline inevitable regardless of promotion.

2

Wanting Without Buying

Consumers want many things they never intend to buy: wanting something is a necessary but not a sufficient reason for buying. This chapter explains why buying does not occur even when there is an underlying want for the product. By understanding this concept, we are in a better position to understand buying itself.

A want may remain dormant or inactive for one or more of the following reasons:

- The want for the product is *latent:* The want is dormant until awakened by the consumers' becoming aware of what the product can really do for them.
- The want is *passive:* Although consumers are aware of the product's potential benefits and are conscious of wanting the product, they are inhibited from buying by an objective assessment of benefits and costs.
- There are *exclusionary* reasons for not buying: Exclusionary reasons for not buying relate to consumers' ethical or legal reasons or incapacities.

LATENT WANTS

A latent want remains dormant unless consumers are made aware of the product's potential for meeting their goals. The key here is knowledge of potential since just being aware of the product's existence is not enough. In fact, consumers may be aware of a product's existence and be able to recognize it and identify it by name, while still not realizing the product's potential for meeting their goals. As a consequence, there is no conscious want for the product unless consumers come to realize what the product can do for them.

The concept of latent wants finds expression in that favorite example told by advertising agents about Elias Howe, the inven-

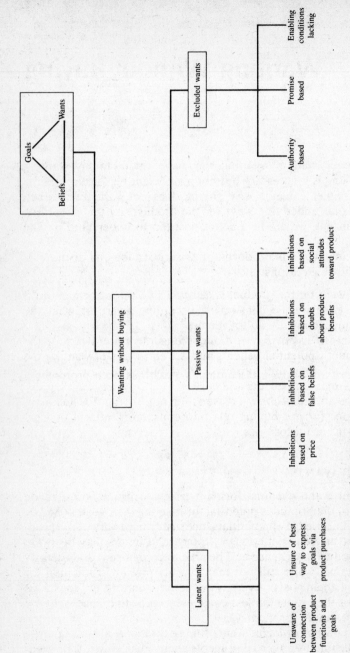

Figure 4 Reasons for Wanting Without Buying

tor of the sewing machine, who died impoverished because he failed to advertise the benefits of the machine. There are two explanations for latent wants:

1. Consumers may know about the product but lack an understanding of either the product's functions or the significance of the function for achieving their goals. The want remains latent and unrealized until the consumer becomes aware of exactly what the product is capable of doing. The situation is analogous to that of sailors in a previous age who had scurvy. The sailors knew about the existence of limes but did not know that the Vitamin C contained in the limes would correct their problem. In this sense, the sailors' latent want for limes would be activated when they were made aware of the connection between the Vitamin C in limes and its effectiveness in curing scurvy.

A product may have many uses that remain unknown unless they are advertised. It is common for a product that has been in decline for one use to be rejuvenated when promoted for another use. For example, while Listerine was initially promoted as a general antiseptic, it has, at various times, been promoted as a cure for bad breath, a cure for dandruff, an after-shave lotion, a sore throat remedy, a reducer of tooth plaque, and a deodorant. Similarly, Fleischmann's Yeast has been promoted not only for baking bread, but as a vitamin supplement and a laxative.

2. Consumers may understand a product's function, but their potential want for the product may remain latent because of doubts about the best way of expressing their goals. For example, seeing the Olympic Games on TV always leads to a dramatic increase in the sales of equipment for the less popular sports like archery and canoeing. Of course, these new buyers already knew of these sports. What was changed by the TV demonstration was the consumer's beliefs about how best to express the life goals that relate to entertainment. A less dramatic illustration occurs whenever advertising puts across the idea that the "good life" demands a second car, a third telephone, a special watch for evening wear, and so on.

An article in the *New York Times* activated the speaker's latent want for a Sony ICF-7600D synthesized receiver in the following extract from a consumer protocol statement. The arti-

cle showed the product's potential for meeting the speaker's goal
of giving order to events by keeping up with home news while
abroad.

> Although I travel a great deal throughout the world, I had never
> bothered taking a radio as I would not be able to follow the news
> in a foreign language and I seldom listen to popular music. How-
> ever, I came across an article in the *New York Times* about what
> one foreign correspondent takes with him on his travels. He men-
> tioned he would never be without his compact Sony synthesized
> receiver that allowed him to keep in touch with English language
> news broadcasts wherever he was in the world. Even if he were in
> China he could get English news broadcasts from the U.S. or Brit-
> ain by simply programming the appropriate wavelength (obtain-
> able from a book supplied with the receiver). The possibility of
> keeping in day-to-day touch with world news suddenly excited me
> as I recalled how often I had felt cut off from what was happening
> in the world. The next day I went out and bought the Sony.

It does not matter whether new product wants acquired
through advertisements are regarded as activated latent wants or
as newly created wants. The fact is, in a society with advancing
affluence and technology, an explosion of new product wants
inevitably occurs. New products come along that provide better
ways to solve old problems at the same time they uncover new
problems for which they claim to be a solution. If the state of
affairs described by higher level goals finds expression in a mul-
titude of possible want categories, it is also true that the want
categories themselves can find expression in an infinite number
of possible products. The potential number of products that
could express higher level goals is only limited by man's
ingenuity.

The truly innovative product constitutes a novel expression
of a goal, just as live TV news expresses in a novel way people's
desire to know what is happening in the world. Not all new-to-
the-world products can be revolutionary expressions of wants.
Some significant modifications of existing products arise by acci-
dent, often with a lack of awareness of the significance of the
innovation for the market.

Ivory Soap, which has been on the market for over a century,
has the feature of being able to float in water. This attribute was
discovered accidentally, and there were doubts initially as to
whether such an attribute, if promoted, would sell the product.

Potato chips were discovered in 1853 when a chef reacted to constant customer complaints that the French fries were too thick. Again, it was not immediately obvious that the product would have general appeal.

Tea bags came into being at the beginning of the century when a New York merchant used small silk bags to send samples of tea to his customers. It was the merchant's customers who immediately saw and demanded the convenience of porous bags for making a single cup of tea.

Doubt about the significance of an innovation frequently arises when the innovation is not an improvement in fulfilling what is considered the product's core function. Thus, Kodak rejected the initial Polaroid camera on the ground that it would only be a short-lived fad.

It is often easier to predict a latent want and the corresponding potential demand for a product that is just an incremental, evolutionary, or technological improvement on current products (e.g., *color* TV) than for new products that are in some way discontinuous (e.g., the automobile). Where a new product is discontinuous, consumers often initially doubt the product's worth, dread the costs to be incurred in using it, and perhaps anticipate problems arising from its initial lack of fit to the rest of the consumer's consumption system (i.e., a lack of fit to the existing coordinated set of purchases that reflects the consumer's lifestyle).

Customers themselves often suggest ideas for product improvement. There is usually someone out there with the imagination to visualize the perfect solution and to use this as a standard against which to detect imperfections in even the best of current offerings. Procter and Gamble's Tide, the first heavy-duty detergent, resulted from the company's attempt to fulfill the expressed wish of many housewives for a detergent that would clean effectively without leaving curdle-like foam in the wash. But customers are less likely to suggest truly innovative products that tap some latent want.

PASSIVE WANTS

All buying can be seen as an approach-avoidance situation—there are approach factors (attractions) in buying as well as avoidance factors (costs). Avoidance factors either inhibit purchase altogether or, at the very least, reduce buying enthusiasm. Where buying is inhibited, the want for the product is said to be passive. Consumers with a passive want for a product are aware of the product and its potential benefits for them, but they believe the avoidance factors outweigh the approach factors. Whereas in the case of a latent want the consumer is not even conscious of wanting the product, in the case of a passive want the consumer is aware of wanting it. However, because of other factors, the consumer does not want the product enough to buy it.

Although "passive" suggests "sitting back" in some way, this need not be so. For instance, someone held back from buying by price may search for the product at a lower price as the following extracts from buying protocols make clear:

> I expect I'll buy my "Opium" cologne soon. I want it and love its scent. I have the money and am well able to afford it but the parsimonious habits of a lifetime are holding me back from the actual purchase. I regard it an an extravagance—sheer luxury—so I continue to shop around to get it for the lowest possible price.

In the next protocol statement, the consumer has a passive want for a king-size bed, but is inhibited from buying by price:

> Originally, I couldn't make my mind up about what sort of bed I wanted—for example, twin, queen or king size. I only knew I didn't want a double bed. I had always cherished an ambition to have a king-size bed but shied away from these after I saw the prices.
>
> I had to wait for my husband to come with me to buy the bed because only he had a check! We happened first to go into Kingston's. Their furniture department was very small but what they had was on sale. We looked at some divans, twin size, which seemed to be reasonably priced and a good buy. If I had been alone I would have bought them. However, my husband was very interested in the king size, which was also on sale. He pointed out the false economy of buying a cheap bed. This, together with my sneaking ambition to have a king size, decided me.

The passive want for a king-size bed was activated by the husband dealing with his wife's objection to spending so much money on a bed. He helped change her mind about the importance of price by relating it to corresponding benefits: value for money, not cheapness per se, should be the rule for buying the bed. In actual fact, the wife only needed an excuse for buying a king-size bed, so the husband's endorsement of the purchase plus any reasonable argument undermining her objection might have led her to the purchase. A salesperson in the store might have been equally as effective as the husband in persuasion, but the husband's endorsement might have been necessary to tip the scales.

Inhibitors might include price, false or true beliefs, doubts about the claims made, and social norms. A latent want can develop into a passive want instead of an active want if such inhibitors remain as barriers.

Price

Price can inhibit buying not because the price demanded is beyond the consumer's ability to pay (which would take him or her out of the market entirely), but because the price is more than the consumer is willing to spend. The problem lies in the relative benefits the consumer attaches to the product versus the money, which can be spent on other things. Anything that minimizes the impact of price (e.g., easy credit terms) or the importance attached to price (e.g., getting the consumer to treat price as an investment rather than a payment) will alter the relative weight given to money and related matters.

False Beliefs

The price to the consumer may seem high in relation to benefits (with the consequence that buying is inhibited) when, in fact, the evaluation of benefits rests on *false beliefs*. Thus, there may be many people who want a home computer but do not buy because they believe that learning to use one would be much too difficult. This is a common problem for manufacturers. The solution is to demonstrate the falseness of the belief. Doretta Steinway got the sales of Steinway pianos off the ground by offering free piano lessons to purchasers. Singer, in its early sewing machine days, had a problem convincing women they could ever learn to use a sewing machine. The solution was to employ young girls as demonstrators while offering free lessons with each purchase.

The various advertised "torture" tests to which Timex watches were subjected (e.g., a Timex watch attached to the outboard engine propeller of a speedboat) were designed to dispel false beliefs about cheap watches being unable to withstand tough treatment. ("Timex takes a licking and keeps on ticking.")

In Britain, false beliefs about houses with timber frames continue to inhibit the purchase of such houses in spite of government research demonstrating that timberframe houses catch fire no more frequently then brick.

False beliefs often resist change. This is partly because false beliefs are apt to be part of a system of beliefs—so that false beliefs must be eradicated within a whole set of related beliefs rather than individually. Thus, the consumer does not just begin to believe that timber-frame houses are as good as brick houses. Instead, the consumer begins to believe a whole host of other propositions about housing, such as the durability of wooden structures, and so on. It is because the individual belief about a product, feature or attribute is part of a system of beliefs that an extreme attack on the one belief can stimulate robust rebuttal based on these other beliefs while mere doubts raised about the individual belief may be accommodated without any change in beliefs.

False beliefs (eg., about how to order one's life) can also be a reason for a want being latent. However, there is a difference: consumers are not conscious of their latent wants, but they are aware of their passive wants.

True Beliefs

A consumer may be held back from buying by true beliefs about the pros and cons of buying. For example, in the early days of contact lenses many people who wanted their benefits were put off by the known discomfort they caused. The manufacturers either had to get the consumer to perceive the discomfort as minor (which might be very difficult to do) or had to develop a more comfortable product, which they did by creating soft lenses.

Some beliefs that inhibit buying are neither true nor false at the time they are held, but are simply beliefs about the future. For example, consumers often believe that products currently on the market are likely to be quickly superseded by something better and/or cheaper. Such beliefs are common in respect to new electronics products from video cassette recorders (VCRs) to computers. However, postponement of buying means not only a consumption delay, but the sacrifice of various social rewards associated with being among the first to own the product.

Doubts About Claims

The consumer may consciously want a product but be held back by doubts. Doubting a claim is different from disbelieving a claim. If I disbelieve the claim that product X will cure cancer, then I believe that product X will not cure cancer. However, if I doubt the claim I am simply saying I am uncertain as to whether to believe or disbelieve the claim.

Doubts about advertised claims abound. In particular, consumers have learned from experience to discount claims about "revolutionary" advances over the competition. Since such doubts can impede the adoption of truly major innovations, they need to be anticipated and dispelled. When General Foods brought out Maxim, its freeze-dried coffee, it anticipated consumer doubts about whether an instant coffee would taste almost like real coffee and chose to reduce the credibility gap by advertising the manufacturing process. When the Cuisinart was first shown, there was a danger of its being dismissed as a sort of souped-up blender—except for the efforts of a group of influential chefs who promoted the food processor's unique advantages.

Consumers often have doubts about multi-use products performing as well in each individual use as a product designed specifically for that purpose. Uses that are in addition to some perceived core use for a product may be treated by the consumer as neither the best use for the product nor the best product for the use. When multi-use products are bought they are likely to be bought for their versatility (and usual cost saving), but where there is no viable market segment based on versatility, the seller might find it more advantageous to focus on the major, more profitable use.

Associated with consumer skepticism about multi-use products there are frequently suspicions that product advances in one direction may mean losses elsewhere. ("It stands to reason something's got to give.") One advertisement for Mop and Glo, a floor cleaner that claims a high shine on floors without making them slippery, anticipated customer reactions by showing how one housewife's doubts were removed by a visit to a friend's house. Also, just as people may not expect a product to be equally good in each of its several uses, they may doubt whether a firm can be equally as successful across a wide range of product categories. Some firms capitalize on this by stressing their specialized nature (e.g., Gerber's one-time slogan "Babies are our business. Our only business"). Other firms seek to get round the potential bias by the adoption of individual brand names. A company name may not carry over to other products unless there is a *strong* family resemblance in terms of exploiting the firm's known competence even if it is just snob appeal. As one customer said in a protocol statement: "Buying a TV from G.E. does not sit well with me. I think of G.E. more for refrigerators, dishwashers, and light bulbs—but not TVs."

Social Norms

Another inhibitor is social norms. As purchases signal the buyer's rank, values, and preferred self image, to the world, it follows that purchases should be *socially supportive*. A consumer may want—or even need—something but the purchase can be proscribed or at least discouraged by social norms. The sales of hearing aids have been less than would be anticipated given the real need for them because wearing one detracts from the social self. The development of less visible aids has helped sales, although for many people the potential embarrassment is still there. Perhaps the wearing of a hearing aid by President Reagan reduces their social liability.

Social factors inhibit sales of cosmetics to men. One firm trying to get around this employs a macho, cigar-smoking star in their advertisements, rejecting the label of cosmetics in favor of the phrase "skin fitness and bath products." By conjuring up associations of "skin fitness" and manliness, the firm hopes to change perceptions enough to counter social inhibitions.

Even when a purchase is not going to be highly visible in the individual's social world, consumers often act as if big (social) brother is watching them. Sometimes, there is conflict in the demands of different groups (e.g., family norms about dress and the teenagers' social group), so the final decision must resolve many internal conflicts.

In general, advertising that violates social or group norms, rules, or standards will find difficulty winning acceptance. When the norms are not an integral part of the relevant social group's way of life, it is difficult to make them so. The attempts by the coffee industry to increase sales by trying to persuade the younger generation that coffee fits into their lifestyle has had very limited success. Ultimately, it is the reality of experience—not advertising—that shapes such perceptions. Advertising, however, may shape perceptions by augmenting or transforming relevant experience.

EXCLUDED WANTS

A consumer can consciously want a product but *exclude* the want from consideration for certain exclusionary reasons. *Exclusionary reasons* for not buying a product have nothing to do with *buying* goals. They are reasons that refer to perceived ethical or legal obligations or to incapacities that remove the consumer from the market (Raz, 1975).

Authority-Based Factors

Consumers may defer to some authority, such as the government or church, and refrain from buying. Whenever the consumer accepts the authority's rules as legitimate demands and such rules prohibit buying products, people feel obligated to take themselves out of the market. Thus several religious groups condemn the buying and consumption of liquor, while in certain states people may refrain from buying guns because of local laws.

Promise-Based Factors

A consumer may promise not to buy a particular product. For example, teenagers may promise their parents not to buy a motorcycle.

Apart from any sanctions, breaking of such a promise results in guilt and anxiety. Keeping the promise reinforces commitment.

Lack of Enabling Conditions

The consumer may not be able to use the particular product due to a lack of enabling conditions. The consumer may suffer some disability that prevents him from using the product or he may lack complementary facilities. For example, a person may want some electrical appliance like an automatic washing machine but may not have the needed electricity in the home, and so on.

One very important enabling condition is having enough money to buy the product. However, price as an exclusionary reason should be distinguished from price as an inhibitor of buying. When price inhibits buying (so that the want remains passive), it means simply that the consumer is not prepared to pay the price, although he or she is capable of doing so. In contrast, when price is an exclusionary reason, the consumer does not have and cannot get the money to buy the product.

Exclusionary reasons override personal preferences. Marketing is usually ineffective in removing the barrier of exclusionary reasons as the consumer is already "sold" on the product but obligations and incapacities prevent acting on the want. However, although the consumer is not a buying prospect, he or she remains a buying suspect in case circumstances change.

SUMMARY

Wanting a product is not a sufficient reason for buying it. In the first place, a want may be *latent* in that consumers are unaware of the connection between the product and what it can do for them. A latent want for a product may be aroused by making consumers aware of what the product can do for them or getting consumers to perceive the product as a better way to express their goals. In the second place, a want may be *passive* in that consumers are held back from buying because costs seem to outweigh benefits. A passive want for a product may be aroused by overcoming consumer objections. This is generally a better strategy than seeking to enhance current perceptions of acknowledged benefits if the consumer is to buy wholeheartedly and not at the expense of anxiety. A latent want may on occasion develop into a passive want unless objections are overcome. Finally, consumers may have *exclusionary reasons* for not buying. Exclusionary reasons refer to moral or legal obligations or incapacities that to all intents and purposes take the consumer out of the market.

Note: We have assumed in this chapter that what is wanted is available. This may not be the case. The consumer may have a frustrated want for some product or product features not yet in existence. Inquiries aimed at identifying such wants can be a source of ideas for product improvements and new product development.

IMPLICATIONS FOR MARKETING

1. Where the level of market penetration represents only a small proportion of prospects, the firm should check whether those *not* buying
   (a) Are aware not just of the firm's brand but what it can do for them as the want may be *latent*.

   (b) Are aware of the product's benefits but are inhibited from buying in that the want is *passive*.

   (c) Have *exclusionary* reasons that exclude them from the market.

2. If prospective customers do not fully understand or realize the potential benefits of the firm's brand, the firm needs to demonstrate the link between brand and want and/or show how the brand promotes some not-to-be neglected way of achieving the good life. This may require repositioning the brand.

3. If prospective customers are inhibited from buying the firm's products, the firm should identify the source of the inhibition and judge whether it is feasible and commercially viable to seek via its communications (e.g., personal selling) to overcome the objection viz:

Objection	Promotional Focus
Price	To minimize the impact (e.g., offer of credit) or perceptions of importance (e.g., suggesting the price is an investment).
False beliefs	To change or mould the system of beliefs of which the false belief is a part.
True beliefs	To depreciate the importance of the objection *or* to compensate for the value of the objection.
Doubts	To remove the doubt by showing it is either untenable or nonapplicable.
Contrary to social norms	To demonstrate social approval by significant others or depreciate the importance of the lack of social approval.

4. In considering additional new products, a firm should recognize that there are potentially an infinite number of products for which there are latent wants so that creativity in marketing is all important.

5. Where certain customers have exclusionary reasons for not buying the firm's product, they are out of the market and hence not part of any calculation of market potential unless there is evidence that these reasons will change.

3

Buying as Rule-Following Behavior

When a consumer wants a product and is not held back from buying (i.e., the want is not latent, passive, or excluded) the want plus beliefs about the various brands being considered constitute the *reasons* for buying a particular brand. It is argued that whenever consumers act for reasons, their actions are intentional and planned, which implies that certain rules are followed. When consumers act for reasons, they act "as if" they are following rules.

INTENTIONAL BUYING ACTION AND REASONS FOR PURCHASE

Social life requires understanding other people's behavior. We constantly interpret the actions of others as a basis for responding to them. We think that we can understand others because we attribute rationality to their actions. Without apparent rationality, people's behavior seems abnormal or even insane. In finding rationality in what others do, we conclude that what they did was a "reasonable thing to do" given their wants and beliefs.

Buying behavior is both intentional and rational, although perhaps less rational than assumed by most economic models. We can contrast intentional action with involuntary behavior. Intentional action is purposeful, voluntary, and meaningful. It is something done *by*—rather than *to*—a person.

Consumers buy what they want to buy providing there are no stronger reasons against buying. Their reasons for buying embrace "whatever consideration induced, inclined, weighed with or decided them to buy" (Beck, 1975). These reasons must be intelligible to other people if they are to count as reasons, otherwise the behavior tends to be regarded as involuntary or a mistake ("no one in his right mind would do that"). There is little room in this viewpoint for the psychoanalytic claim that the springs of human action are largely unconscious and that people are not always even aware of why they act as they do (Gay, 1985), at least not in respect to intentional buying.

Consumers buy the brands they believe are the most efficient and socially appropriate for meeting their wants (Peters, 1958). Both social appropriateness and efficiency matter. Thus, although a goat may be more efficient than a lawn mower in keeping a lawn trim, it is not a solution that would be considered socially appropriate in the suburbs and, for this reason, is unlikely to be adopted.

Intentional buying action is always purposeful. An intentional explanation of a consumer's choice of brand should thus show:

- What goals or wants the choice of brand was intended to serve.
- The relevant beliefs held by the consumer. An intentional explanation of brand choice should demonstrate the buyer not only acted *with* a reason but *for* the reasons given. Intentional explanations assume that buying actions are conscious actions: to have an intention is to have a want in mind while to act on the intention is to have a belief that the contemplated actions will meet the want.

The reasons lying behind intentional buying action can be classified into operative reasons and auxiliary reasons (Raz, 1975):

- Operative reasons refer to goals/wants.
- Auxiliary reasons refer to the choice criteria used to evaluate alternative brands.

A consumer's reasons for buying a particular brand are *conclusive* if they lead to the buying of the brand. However, for all practical purposes, such reasons are never *absolute:* brand loyalty is always conditional. There are always circumstances, such as a price increase or the entry into the market of a better substitute, that would lead the consumer to switch brands.

THE CONCEPT OF RULE FOLLOWING

An extension of the idea of acting for reasons is acting "as if" in accordance with rules. Although the idea that intentional action as planned action follows rules is not new to this century, interest in this topic was revived and sustained in the 1950s and 1960s by philosophers and social scientists such as Winch (1958), Von Wright (1962), R. Taylor (1966), Harré and Secord (1973), C. Taylor (1964), and Shwayder (1965).

A rule is an instruction, consciously or unconsciously followed, stating what is to be done in order to achieve the end in view. It is a recipe for a designated achievement (Black 1970). Harré and Secord give the general form of a rule as: "In order to achieve A (the act) do $a_1 \ldots a_n$ (the actions) when S (the occasion or situation) occurs."

Rules may be personal (i.e., the individual's own set of guidelines), social (i.e., conventional rules like those about dress or the marriage ceremony), or institutional (as in the case of a buying department's rules). Whether the rules are personal or social, they are usually followed unconsciously. Consumers know the reasons for their actions, but they are not aware of rules embedded in the reasons.

With social behavior like buying, reasons become more intelligible when seen as part of a set of rules governing buying activities. Even when consumers appear to act randomly, they may still be conforming to some rule, for example,

> "If there is nothing to choose among the brands I'll take any one of them."

Buying as a Performance

In viewing buying behavior as an action that follows rules, we see buying as a performance that can be good or bad according to some rule. Buying actions follow rules because it makes sense to distinguish between right and wrong ways to make buying choices. As long as there is a possibility of making a mistake, buying actions will be guided and constrained by rules designed to avoid mistakes and poor buying decisions.

Rules in buying act like a set of negative and positive rules of thumb that categorize certain actions as being nonpermissible (like buying a "pig in a poke") and permitting those actions that seem to serve as the best means of achieving what is sought. Although rules do not guide the totality of consumer behavior, they do place constraints on both the priorities with which goals are sought and the means adopted for attaining them (Langford, 1971). These rules are not true or false but simply effective or ineffective and correct or incorrect in terms of achieving what is sought. Whenever actions like buying can be said to be performed correctly or incorrectly, it implies there are rules to be followed. Such rules are learned through education and experience and are continued if effective.

The cognitive psychologist refers to such rules as "procedural knowledge" since they are knowledge or beliefs about how to do things like choosing what brand to buy (Anderson, 1983). Some rules evolve from acquiring relevant facts about the rival brands, interpreting such facts in the light of the buying situation, and then modifying the rules as experience develops. This does not, however, imply that buyers are conscious of the rules being followed. Buying actions conform to rules in the sense that actions fit a rule, or rules can describe the behavior without necessarily implying that consumers know the rules underlying their behavior or that they can in any way articulate them. A rule is a description of a regularity in buying behavior. Such rules make sense when examined in conjunction with knowledge of the buying context and the relevant social scene and culture. Both Goffman (1963) and Garfinkel (1967) show that even though a person is not consciously following any set of rules, his or her departure from what is expected elicits the same response from others as that brought forth through a breaking of some formal set of rules.

Content and Structure of Rules

The set of rules covering any particular purchase have both content and structure. While the content of the rules describes goals, wants, beliefs, and choice criteria, the structure of the rules describes how the rules are related in terms of their consistency, mutual coherence, and relative importance. There are different degrees to which rules are consciously followed (Black, 1970).

Buyers Who Invoke Rules

In this case, the buyer actually follows a set of formal instructions or questions that imply instructions such as the following incomplete (and not entirely logical) set of reasons meant to help women choose a dress.

1. Does it really fit? Sit, walk, reach?
2. Does it look great?

3. Do I love it?
4. Do I already have it?
5. If for a specific occasion, will it go beyond?
6. Does it work with two or three things I own?
7. If not, is this the best way to experiment?
8. Is it good value? Consider: quality, versatility, wearability.
9. Even if it is, can I afford it right now?
10. Can I wait for it to go on sale?
11. If it's on sale, would I want (not necessarily buy) it if it weren't?
12. Can I handle the alterations and cleaning costs, if any?
13. Do I have shoes for it?
14. Bonus: Can I wear it nine months of the year?
15. Will I love it next year?
16. Is it so cheap that none of these questions matter?

Buyers Governed by Rules

Here, rules are consciously recalled as when the woman in the last discussion tells the store clerk exactly what sort of dress she is looking for. Consumers often have a standard in mind. This standard can be broken down into a set of rules describing what is sought. Thus, one customer buying a pair of sneakers spoke of New Balance as, "the standard against which I will judge."

Buyers Who Accept Rules

If a buyer does not actively attempt to remember any set of rules, although rules are implicitly being followed, a buyer accepts rules. Thus, people may accurately classify objects without knowing the rules involved and may speak grammatically without being able to recall the rules of grammar.

Intentional buying is, at least, a rule-accepting action (Black, 1970) because

1. Consumers acknowledge having made a mistake and making a mistake implies violating a rule.
2. Each action taken by the consumer can be justified in terms of wants and beliefs that imply that the action is guided by a rule that relates actions to wants and beliefs.
3. It makes sense to say the buying action is not complete up to

any stage prior to purchase, thus implying that intentional buying action involves a plan to meet some want—and a plan always consists of rules.

4. Buying action is purposeful, which means the action is guided by the rule that actions should be in line with purpose.

Consumer Rules and Consumer Roles

The rules followed by a buyer make each action an expression of an underlying intention. Since some rules are tied to ensuring that choices are socially appropriate, this suggests that some rules belong to the fabric of roles adopted by the consumer. With every role there is a set of expectations as to how someone performing that role should behave. For example, a woman in the role of mother is expected to choose nourishing food for her children.

It is argued that people picture themselves in one or more ideal roles. For example, a man may imagine himself in the role of a family man, businessman, handyman, sportsman, and so on, in order to shape his behavior one way or another. While adopting a particular role, a person becomes attracted to what is assumed to go with the role, just as someone fantasizing the role of yachtsman is attracted to the particular look in clothes that seems to go with yachting. But the rules or expectations implicit in a role provide the bare outlines and not a detailed script, allowing room for variation. The rules associated with roles are essentially normative rather than followed to the letter although they usually "impose stylistic elements on performance" (Harré and Secord, 1973).

It is much easier to distinguish right and wrong ways of doing things when the rules are tied to some role (MacIntyre, 1971). But there is a danger of just arbitrarily giving a role name to every distinct buying occasion without evidence that buyers do in fact play different roles on these different occasions. A more pressing question lies in explaining why buyers should give priority to meeting role expectations when this conflicts with self-interest (Ryan, 1978). For example, why should a woman who is buying food for her children give absolute priority to the role of mother? To explain this we need not only to know about the social expectations associated with the role of mother but also about her wants and beliefs.

RULE IDENTIFICATION

How do we go about identifying the rules used by buyers? We need to interpret what the buying means to the buyer. Such an interpretation of meaning is analogous to interpreting a text. The possibility of understanding the consumer, like understanding a written text, rests on the assumption of shared meanings. In the most general terms, the process of rule identification consists of first showing buying actions are the outcome of reasons and then explaining the key words or concepts employed in these reasons to identify the rules they imply. (See Figure 5.) Consider, for example, the following protocol statement made by a woman buying a pair of shoes in New York:

> The shoe must be suitable for my active urban-day life; heels not too high and shoes solid and serviceable. They must be considered "in fashion" by those "in the know" and be recognized as "right" even by those who dislike them.

We might interpret the key concepts in this statement as follows:

Active urban-day life: We interpret this as suited "to being constantly on the go in the city."

Heels not too high: Inquiries about dimensions reveals "shoes with heels around 1½ inches."

Solid and serviceable: Shoes must "stand up to wear and be able to withstand all weather except snow and slush."

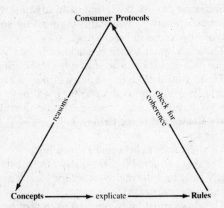

Figure 5   Identifying the Rules Consumers Use in Buying

In fashion by those *in the know:* The shoes should signify to those who follow fashion that they reflect the latest styles.

Recognized as right even by those who dislike them: That those who follow fashion should recognize the shoes as reflecting current styles is more important than that these same people should like the shoes.

To get a deeper feel for what is being said, this respondent's answer might be reworded as follows:

> The shoe should have a 1½ inch heel and be able to stand up to the wear that results from being constantly on the go in the city and be able to withstand all weather except the extreme conditions of snow and slush. Nonetheless, the shoes should signify to those who follow fashion that they reflect current styles and this is more important to me than that these same people should like what I buy.

This consumer's want can be expressed in terms of her reasons, which in turn can be transformed into corresponding rules:

A. **Operative Reasons (Goals, wants, values/beliefs)**
   (a) *Aspiration-level goal.* Signal to others values and self-image.
   (b) *Want.* A pair of shoes that are in fashion but not necessarily the most fashionable.
   (c) *Beliefs*
   - High heels (greater than 1½ inches) are unsuited to an urban life-style.
   - Shoes for day-to-day living in an urban setting must be robust enough to withstand the weather and sidewalks typically found in New York.
   - There are shoes which are acknowledged to be in fashion by a group I consider trendsetters in this area.
   - Those who dislike the shoes will nonetheless not indicate their disapproval since they will have to acknowledge that the shoes reflect one fashion trend.

B. **Auxiliary Reasons (Choice Criteria)**
   (a) *Efficiency*
   - The heel should be about 1½ inch high.
   - The shoes should be of the quality to withstand constant city wear and normal weather for New York City.
   (b) *Social appropriateness*
   - The shoes must be recognized as in fashion.
   - They do not necessarily have to be the shoes every fashion conscious woman would choose.

This consumer is following a rule to the effect that whenever the occasion arises in the foreseeable future in which she needs a pair of shoes for everyday town wear, she will seek to buy a pair that

- Have a 1½ inch high heel.
- Can withstand constant city wear and inclement weather.
- Will be recognized as fashionable by those who are fashion-conscious.

Although the above rules seem straightforward enough, the marketing manager will be interested to know by what *observations* the consumer judges that a shoe could withstand constant city wear and New York weather, as well as the observations used to judge that the shoe will be recognized as fashionable. By knowing what the consumer is looking for the marketing manager can build this into his product and promotions.

The following is a longer protocol recording the thoughts of a consumer as she went about choosing a sewing machine. The reader might try to identify the rules being followed:

Protocol Statement Involving an Infrequent Purchase

This is a major purchase and one with a lot of emotional implications as, if I choose the wrong machine, I am going to feel angry and frustrated for a long time, since a sewing machine should last forever. I therefore decided to shop around carefully. I watched the newspapers for advertisements. I asked friends which machine they would recommend.

One friend who sews a lot was very decisive in her views. "*Definitely* get a *Husqvarna*," she said, "they are marvelous." She went on to describe how satisfied she is with hers. She also went on to tell me about a friend of hers who sews to almost professional standards. This friend bought a Singer and it was "worn out" within a year. She then bought a Husqvarna and has worked happily with it since.

This decided me. I would get Husqvarna—especially since I already had a favorable impression of them—due partly to the advertising campaign. At this point I should mention that it is impossible to judge the quality and special features of a sewing machine by looking at it or even seeing a demonstration (the demonstrators know a few tricks!). One can only judge a machine by using it, and since a certain amount of learning and skill is involved for handling each machine, it really isn't feasible to practice on each machine in the shop. So, on the whole, recommendation by a friend is a fairly good, reliable method of getting what one wants.

The first thing I found was that there aren't many shops selling sewing machines in New York. Singer is well represented but I had already eliminated them from the choice. I had decided that even before I spoke to my friend but that conversation clinched it. This seems strange when I say that I used a Singer for 24 years and found it an excellent machine. My reasons for turning down a Singer are that they now seem "cheap," that is, plastic, gimmicky and expensive, plus the fact that when I went into Singer's to do my "shopping around" I found there were several pushy salesmen hanging about, but when they found I was "only looking" they weren't interested.

I proceeded to look around and found a shop that seemed ideal. They sold several makes including Husqvarna. However, I quickly had to eliminate the Husqvarna from my choice as I found they were around $400 plus. I decided then that I would look for a simpler machine as I didn't really *need* one that would do embroidery. I found one, a 'White.' I had never heard of it but the salesgirl assured me that the name was second only to Singer. This machine was $240 and had all the features I wanted except embroidery. If I had had a checkbook with me, I might have bought it there and then, but I had to say I would think it over. I did look at other machines while I was in the shop, but there was nothing else under $300 with the features I wanted (e.g., zig-zag, stretch stitch, buttonhole).

A few days later (after going to look at Macy's machines and finding they had closed the department) I saw some machines in Gimbel's, all of which had the Gimbel's label. They were on sale and I was amazed at the prices. They were $20 to $60 off the original prices, but even so they were very inexpensive compared with the luxury-priced machines I had seen earlier. I looked at several of these machines and had a demonstration on the ones that interested me.

I told my husband what I had seen and that for $108 I could get a machine that had all the features I required and also it would do embroidery. It was reduced from $180. He said, "Get it—you can always get a more expensive one later." I had already more or less decided that I would get it, since the price was an important factor at this stage, and it did everything I wanted. I got it.

In use, the machine seems good (so far) but I will reserve a final judgment until I have used it with several different kinds of fabrics. I feel pleased about the buy and think I have got a good functional machine.

Protocol Analysis

In order to buy the right sewing machine and avoid the emotional upset arising from a wrong decision, the consumer took account of the following rules:

1. Visit several stores to learn about what sewing machines are available, with what features and at what prices.
2. Look for advertisements in newspapers for special offers on sewing machines.
3. Ask friends who have recently bought sewing machines what they would recommend.
4. Choose a machine that has zig-zag, stretch stitch, and button-hole features, but not necessarily with embroidery features.
5. Preferably buy the Husqvarna brand.
6. Avoid buying any sewing machine that appears cheap and gimmicky as indicated by the thin plastic parts typified by the Singer machine.

The rules form a plan of action for the consumer so she can avoid making a mistake or a poor buying decision. As with plans in general, the rules are not absolute but operate as guidelines. A major concern of the consumer is to avoid the anticipated emotional upset that would arise from buying the wrong machine. However, the consumer's choice criteria with respect to product attributes were too general to make a firm brand choice. The consumer implicitly recognizes this and sees the need for learning through shopping around and taking particular account of the recommendations of friends. A friend's recommendation plus the consumer's own impressions led her to decide to buy the Husqvarna. However, the decision was not unconditional (e.g., reasons for buying were not absolute) and the consumer changed her mind on learning about prices.

The consumer was prepared to infer the level of "goodness" of a brand from what friends had to say about their own experience with the brand. However, some inferences are made from appearances. Thus, the Singer machine was perceived as "cheap" on the grounds that it was plastic and gimmicky.

Lack of familiarity with a brand name was a drawback to its purchase. Thus, the consumer hesitated over the White brand name because she had never heard of it, although she was prepared to be reassured by the salesgirl. Situational factors (not having her checkbook with her) prevented the consumer from buying the White sewing machine. The perception of a bargain-buy was the most influential factor in final brand choice, given that the brand name had all the features that were sought without appearing cheap and gimmicky.

Marketing Implications of the Analysis

If this consumer's behavior is representative of the segment of the market that is of interest to the firm, then certain marketing implications follow:

1. *Product.* Beyond the core use and consideration of product features that are sought, there is the question of ensuring that the firm's product signals quality and avoids being perceived as cheap and gimmicky.
2. *Price.* This is a price-sensitive segment of the market. Price needs to be competitive with price differentials (within the consumer's price range) being seen to reflect differences in value to the consumer.
3. *Promotion.* The evaluation of rival brands is difficult. Hence, a well-known brand name offers reassurance. However, in deciding to buy a sewing machine the consumer does not *simultaneously* decide on which brand to buy. On the contrary, the consumer acknowledges the need to shop around to find out about the brands available and to consult knowledgable friends. This is a learning process to decide choice criteria or the product attributes wanted and their relative importance. During this period, the consumer is likely to be open to persuasion as to what configuration of benefits or product attributes best suits her purposes. Hence the importance of credible and attractive salespeople to describe, explain and recommend the firm's brand at the point of sale.
4. *Distribution.* As a push strategy is needed at the point of sale, an exclusive distribution system would be recommended. As the consumer shops around before choosing, this exclusive distribution policy is not likely to reduce consumer awareness of the brand.
5. *Service.* Since the word-of-mouth recommendation of friends is important, the firm must ensure its post sales service achieves customer satisfaction.

In subsequent chapters we will be developing a model of why people buy which allows us to make a more sophisticated analysis of such protocols.

Recording the Shopping Episode

The whole sequence of actions involved in buying could be termed *the shopping episode:* the constituent actions leading to the act of buying are the *act-action* structure of the episode. (Harré and Secord, 1973.)

The *act-action* structure needs to be understood. Assuming the buyer's actions are intentional—actions done *by* the buyer and not *to* the buyer—the identification of rules involves discovering the meaning of the situation for the buyer by understanding the problem and perplexities confronted. Ideally, the process of rule identification (what Harré and Secord refer to as the *ethogenic process*) involves collecting protocol statements from consumers:

Before they buy: *anticipatory* account
During buying: *contemporaneous* account
After buying: *retrospective* account

The meaning of the situation facing the buyer and the rules being used emerge from an analysis of the key concepts in the protocol statements.

Rules and Reasons as Explanations

There are those who demand more of an explanation than a specification of reasons and the corresponding rules being followed. We will address those people here.

Ideally, we would like to be able to specify the consumer's reasons, the rules followed on account of the reasons, and the reasoning from rules to buying preference on the rather subtle ground that two people starting with the same rules and reaching the same conclusion can arrive by different routes and so have chosen differently (Harman, 1973). At the simplest level, there are the different ways of interpreting a rule in practice. For example, suppose consumers faced with a set of brands that seem all alike follow the rule: "I buy that which is most familiar." But what does "familiar" mean? The brand most currently advertised or the brand known the longest? The choice criteria are slightly different. This could lead to different choices being made by consumers nominally following the same rule.

More generally, consumers may quote the same rules in respect to the choice criteria they intend to apply, but in practice they may disagree on what signs or observations demonstrate the degree to which the attributes they seek are present. Thus, two consumers may claim 'reliability' to be an important criteria in choosing a washing machine. But will they judge reliability on the basis of the same signs or observations? One consumer may choose the brand name as the best sign of reliability, another consumer may rely on price, and yet another may look for the most solid construction. However, while consumers do not always use the same signs to infer a particular attribute, they generally do not make wholly subjective and idiosyncratic inferences.

Knowing the rules and the reasoning involved in applying the rules allows the marketing manager

To understand how consumers choose a brand.

To focus on choice criteria, inference processes, and the degree to which wants and beliefs are firmly held.

To understand what the corresponding actions mean.

Such rules may not be the most rational, but we can see how they make sense for the consumer. Later in the book, we will translate consumer protocols into a general set of categories. One issue that we will mention here, however, is interpreting the protocol statements accurately. After all, there can be several interpretations of a protocol statement reflecting either different interpretations or different levels of understanding.

Reliability of Protocol Statements

There are limits to what consumers can reveal about their thinking or reasoning processes, and there is sharp debate over this issue (Nisbet and Wilson, 1977 versus Miller and Smith, 1978). Ericsson and Simon (1980) provide the best discussion to date about the conditions under which verbal reports can be accepted as reliable data. Given no intent to deceive, people who are asked to think aloud about what they are currently thinking can be considered reliable. There is more likelihood of bias if people are asked to recall from long-term memory. In the language of cognitive psychology used by Ericsson and Simon, we can expect the information in short-term memory to be reported in full, whereas information in long-term memory will be differentially accessible for various reasons.

A problem does remain in identifying justifying reasons that are also truly motivating, but this is no more disturbing than the "impossibility in the physical sciences of knowing for certain whether one's theoretical explanations are correct" (Harré and Secord, 1973). All this means that we should preferably ask consumers to verbalize concurrently with the prebuying, buying, and post-buying stages so that the verbalizations occur simultaneously with the thought processes generated by the purchasing process. On the basis of the Ericsson and Simon argument, verbalizations of reasons are more likely to be deficient when action is simply a matter of habit. This is because the reasons for habitual choice are not likely to be in short-term memory at the time of purchase. This seems to be a reasonable supposition, although consumers do appear to be able to say what led them to choose the product in the first place although this could sometimes be a rationalization.

Ericsson and Simon stress the importance of interpreting protocol statements in the light of the circumstances (i.e., the buying situation) under which they were obtained. This means that those recording the anticipatory, contemporaneous, and retrospective accounts should also note possible unconscious influences on the respondent's behavior. Yet another check that might aid reliability is allowing the respondent to review the marketer's interpretation of the protocol. A good interpretation is likely to be endorsed by the respondent together, perhaps, with an acknowledgment that the interpretation has even clarified the action for the respondent himself.

No investigative technique is free from potential bias. Just as we can misinterpret what we observe or bias behavior by our conduct or presence during an experiment, so too can testimony be biased. There is always a need for vigilance and a willingness to discard protocols that may be biased.

SUMMARY

An extension of the idea of acting for reasons is that of acting "as if" conforming to a set of rules. Buying actions can be said to follow rules in that it makes sense to the consumer to distinguish between right and wrong ways of going about buying to avoid making either mistakes or poor buying decisions. Consumers are not necessarily aware of conforming to any set of rules. Just as people can speak grammatically without being able to spell out the rules, rules in buying may be followed without being known. We identify the rules being followed by consumers by listening to their reasons at the time of buying and explicate the concepts employed in these reasons to identify the rules being followed. The rules of major interest to the marketing manager are those rules that reflect the choice criteria used in brand choice.

IMPLICATIONS FOR MARKETING

1. In order to incorporate into the firm's marketing strategy the motivations of the consumer, the firm should identify the reasons (i.e., wants and beliefs) lying behind the consumer's actions and intentions.

2. To identify these reasons, the firm should ask members of the market segment to think aloud:
   (a) Before they buy.
   (b) During their purchase.
   (c) After they have bought.

3. The protocol statement should be analyzed and interpreted by identifying the key words used by the respondent as reflecting the motivational reasons at work. Thus in the statement, "I preferred brand X because it was the most *familiar,*" the key focus for identifying reasons at work is the word "familiar."

4. The firm should explicate the concepts reflecting the consumer's reasons to identify the rules or regularities to which the consumer conforms. Thus in the notion of "familiarity" is the rule "other things remaining equal, I buy that which is most familiar."

5. The firm should focus on the reasons or rules that reflect the choice criteria used by the consumer together with the rules by which the consumer moves from choice criteria to establishing the degree to which the product or brand matches choice criteria.

6. To try and ensure that interpretations of protocol statements are reliable and valid, the rules should be tested to see if they make sense in terms of the particular culture or subculture; fit the circumstances at the time of purchase and are generally endorsed by the respondent.

4

Choosing Without Deciding and Choice Without Decision

Product or brand choices are neither true nor false but good or bad, wise or foolish, or effective or ineffective in relation to what is sought. When the consumer finds the making of wise, good, or effective choices to be unproblematic, the resulting selection is an act of mere *choosing*. Such choosing entails little or no deliberation about either goal priorities or the likely costs and benefits attached to the various brand options.

Choosing contrasts with *decision-making,* where choice involves deliberation in making up one's mind on a selection from among the options. Consumer decision-making involves deciding-to-buy something as a result of deciding that such and such is the case. Whereas deciding-to-buy something (e.g. a particular brand) is never a matter of being true or false, deciding that such and such is the case (e.g., that a certain product class is suitable) concerns true or false facts.

While I can decide today to buy a Hoover vacuum cleaner tomorrow, or decide tomorrow whether to buy a Hoover cleaner, it makes no sense to say "I will decide tomorrow that I will buy a Hoover vacuum cleaner" since the statement entails the decision having already been made. In other words, tomorrow's choices may only be known today if a decision has already been made. In other words, consumers cannot say what their decisions will be before they have made them. Once we accept that an individual's decisions, by definition, cannot be known in advance, then it makes no sense to speak of programmed decisions. A programmed decision suggests tomorrow's decision can be known today by running a program that gives the answer. However, this is only so when the word "decision" is very loosely defined as a synonym for choice or selection. For our purposes, the word "decision" will be used only when associated with buying that requires deliberation because of uncertainties regarding the costs and benefits attached to the various options. This does not rule out our trying to forecast decisions by anticipating what considerations are likely to weigh most heavily with the decision maker or, alternatively, asking consumers how they would decide today if they had to do so and just assuming today's decision will be the same tomorrow.

Choices do not necessarily emanate from any decision-making process. They may arise from:

Habit: Choice based on past practice or loyalty.
Picking: Choice based on whim or some random process.
Intrinsic preference: Choice based purely on subjective appeal.

Many purchases are based on habit, picking, or intrinsic preference. (See Figure 6.) These purchases involve little, if any, search for information or evaluation of alternative brands in order to decide what to select.

HABIT

A good deal of buying involves the habitual purchase of the same brand. With habit, past choices act as precedents for future purchases. Product or brand choices based on habit can be distinguished from those based on convention. Choices based on convention (e.g., a white wedding dress) emanate from the process of socialization. We grow up following certain cultural conventions and we acquire others from our social milieu. In con-

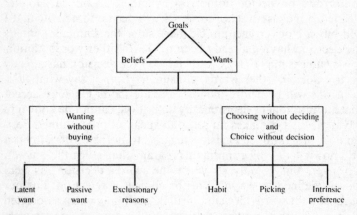

Figure 6   Wanting Without Buying: Choices Without Deciding

trast, choices based on habit result from some initial learning about the product. Consumers may not always accurately recall the reasons lying behind an initial choice. However, they may come to believe that the reasons justifying their past actions are also the reasons that motivate their present choices.

Strength of Habit

Past choices develop into habitual choices with different degrees of commitment. Consumers can just "fall into" a habit or can be completely "sold" on whatever they buy. In the extreme, they might even remain loyal to a brand in the sense of sticking with it through "thick and thin" in spite of evidence that should encourage them to reconsider their choice.

The expression "to fall into a habit" suggests that people may take little effort in making the initial choice that becomes the basis for future choices. There are several reasons why such habits are nonetheless perpetuated:

- People do not wish to deliberate about every purchase.
- Consumers like to reduce the risk of unpleasant surprises (although this is not to suggest risks are avoided at all costs).
- Consumers save time spent on comparative shopping.
- Consumers ensure consistency and reliability in benefits.
- Consumers reaffirm the wisdom of past choices.
- Satisfaction with the past choice reinforces the habit.

As habitual buying develops, the consumer acquires a disposition to go on buying the same brand as before. As the expression goes, people get "set in their ways." However, habitual buying is meaningful behavior and not just a blind, automatic response to a want-stimulus. Consumers can and do remind themselves of the reasons they believe initially led them to patronize the brand. These reasons may lead the consumer to reassess the wisdom of continuing to buy the same brand. The consumer is conscious of being free to act differently and there are inclinations to do so when, for example, the consumer perceives a better offer.

Consumers who fall into the habit of buying a particular brand may not necessarily be well-satisfied with it. They may simply believe that the difficulty or cost of change (information gathering, trial and error learning, and so on) outweighs the likely gains. For example,

> I am not satisfied with my bank. Everyone I deal with there acts as if they are doing you a favor. Errors persist until you finally want to scream. I'd change but it's such a hassle and New York banks are all notoriously bad.

There is also a situation where there are no reasonable alternatives to that being offered and the consumer is unwilling to forego the product (e.g., public transportation).

Being Sold on a Brand

Habitual buying, of course, may arise because the consumer is really "sold" on the brand. A consumer who is sold on a brand is highly satisfied with it: the brand meets expectations in the functions for which it was bought, though this is not to suggest he or she is not open to persuasion, for example

> Nike's have everything I want in a running shoe. I will continue buying them unless I am convinced that some of the other new brands that are coming out make a better running shoe.

Brand Loyalty

Habitual buying may or may not result in significant brand loyalty. Although the term "loyalty" is often used in marketing so as to be indistinguishable from habitual buying, the term, as borrowed from interpersonal relations, clearly implies sticking to a friend through "thick and thin." Using this restricted definition, brand loyalty would apply only to those consumers who stick to a brand even when it is at an overall disadvantage vis-à-vis rival brands. There are consumers who are loyal to brands in this sense:

> Yes, I agree Virgin Atlantic Airline is offering a better deal but I'd feel bad about going with them after People Express has been so good to me.

Most consumers probably have no such loyalty for any brand, and manufacturers should not depend on brand loyalty. Where loyalty does occur, it is more likely that a relationship has become personalized so that change has emotional overtones (e.g., with personal services such as hairdressing). However, this is not to suggest that being loyal in the sense of sticking to a brand through thick and thin must necessarily be emotionally based. There are often hard-headed objective reasons that reinforce tendencies to brand loyalty, as well as emotional or affective supports (Zajonc and Markus, 1982). Consumers will generally switch to a new brand that holds out a wider promise of satisfaction. If the consumer does not do so, it is usually because the perceived cost of change outweighs the perceived advantages or because the individual consumer lacks an educated confidence in being able to recognize a better deal—and not because the consumer feels obligated to be loyal to a "friend."

Brand Switching

Habits are often said to be undermined by a desire for variety and not just by perceptions of a better deal. Manufacturers recognize this motive by providing a variety of designs, flavors, and so on to satisfy the desire for variety without the need to switch brands.

However, switching back and forth between brands does not always arise from variety seeking. The habitual buyer of a brand will occasionally be tempted to try a rival brand, for example, if the price is lower. When the new brand is found to be no better, this type of buyer returns to the original brand. The key point to remember is that the brand habitually bought need not offer _any_ objective advantage over the rival brand. This is because the habitual purchase always has an advantage over any rival that is objectively equivalent. Because the consumer has had longer experience with the habitually bought brand, it has acquired more familiarity and legitimacy and there is more confidence in it and liking for it. Perhaps it is recognition of such behavior that gave rise to the idea of brand loyalty.

Brand Inertia

Writers on buyer behavior refer to "self-perception" theory which says that consumers will attribute their habitual use to something and that this something is often the belief that they really like the brand. This gives rise to brand inertia. Although the marketing literature stresses the short life cycle of products and brands, some brands have been habitual buys from generation to generation for over a hundred years with little change in the product except perhaps in packaging; think of these perennials:

Ivory Soap
Vaseline Petroleum Jelly
Dickinson's Witch Hazel
Arm and Hammer Baking Soda
Bacardi Rum
Heinz Tomato Ketchup
Maxwell House Coffee

Although buying habits can be strong, there are also pressures leading to their being broken:

● People seek more effective or more efficient ways to meet wants.
● People like to appear to be open to new ideas.
● People like variety.
● People experience changes in circumstances, such as marriage.
● People are aware of well-publicized substitutes.

Some of these factors are always at work influencing the consumer to turn away from habit.

Retaining Customers

Manufacturers seek to retain their habitual customers while trying to convert those who buy rival brands. In retaining customers, the aim is to build up resistance to change by convincing users that they are already buying the best. Sometimes, the firm's offering is so improved that customers have a reason other than past precedent for continuing to buy the brand.

It is easier to retain customers than it is to convert them. One reason for this is that consumers want to believe they are already buying or have bought the best. Although they may feel a duty to themselves to periodically consider rival brands, consumers often follow an evaluation process that merely rationalizes why their past choices should be continued. Habitual buyers of a brand may cite reasons for buying that simply repeat advertising slogans for the brand. They also rate advertising for the brand more favorably than that for rival brands. Where this is so, advertising has achieved its goal of getting the consumer to think about and judge the brand in the way suggested by its advertising.

Converting Customers

This discussion of retaining regular customers provides some insight into the problem of converting from rivals. There is no long-term advantage to converting a consumer unless the firm creates a customer and not just a one-off sale. However, one-shot incremental sales may be all that can be expected when there is no significant differentiation among rival brands. Where customers are tempted to try a rival brand by exaggerated promises, they may return to their original brand with a reinforced determination not to stray again on the ground that "once bitten twice shy."

Ideally, converting from rivals should be based on a sustainable critical advantage. A critical advantage is different from a competitive advantage. A competitive advantage is in danger of labeling any differences between the firm's brand and the rival's brand an "advantage." In contrast, a critical advantage is a unique and sustainable advantage that is of central importance to the function for which the consumer is buying the product. A critical advantage may relate to the product itself, to price, to promoted image, to service, or to distribution.

It is easy to confuse a unique advantage with one that is critical to the consumer. Centrality plus uniqueness are needed to establish a critical advantage. Thus, while air safety may be of central importance to air travellers, it is not critical if all airlines are perceived as having equivalent safety records. Similarly, a steak dinner on the flight to Florida may be unique but hardly of central concern to passengers. Consumers must continue to regard the advantage as central with competitors not being able or willing to copy it.

Protocol Statement Involving a Habitual Purchase

We will now analyze a protocol statement involving a habitual purchase. Following the recommendations of Chapter 3, the protocol is divided into the anticipatory, contemporaneous, and retrospective accounts.

Illustrative Protocol Statement

Anticipatory Account

I intend to buy Palmolive dishwashing liquid. I am very conscientious about my hands. They have to look the best at all times, so I select a detergent which cares about my hands and gives good performance. I have tried Joy, Lux, Octagon, and many others. Palmolive is the one I like best. I have no hesitation about going to the counter and putting it in my grocery basket.

Palmolive is very soft to my hands. I can wash umpteen dishes with it and my hands are still soft. One thing I cannot tolerate is rough and ruddy hands. The first thing one notices in a woman is her hands. I don't even use hand lotion after washing. Also, I save money because I can do many dishes and still have suds. I have suds remaining to clean greasy cast iron skillets and frying pans. With other detergents I found that you can only do four or five dishes and then have to add more detergent. My dishes are clean and shiny after using only one squirt of Palmolive.

Every time a new detergent comes out they send me samples in the mail. I use the samples because I don't like to waste anything and I like to try new things. But none have outperformed Palmolive. You know, I used to use Octagon all the time until I got a Palmolive sample. Octagon comes in a big bottle, but it keeps losing its suds. The large economy size was not as economical as I thought. I used Joy, but it was rough on my hands and made them itch. They brag about Ivory being soft to the hands, but my hands were very itchy and sensitive after using it.

My friends at work also use Palmolive. Even my mother uses it—she is 78 years old and suffers from arthritis. I even like their TV ad with Madge who has her customers soak their hands in Palmolive!

Contemporaneous Account

I am buying this Palmolive (32 ounces) with confidence. I used to buy this junk Octagon. You need all 48 ounces to wash your dishes; I don't care if it is economically priced.

I have tried the majority of these brands. Joy is too strong for my hands and Octagon is sudless. Ivory is more expensive than

Palmolive and is not as good. I'd probably buy Ivory, though, if they didn't have Palmolive. But I am not overly impressed with Ivory's cleaning. They sure do advertise a lot! It's foolish for me to pay more when I like Palmolive.

It is the prettiest bottle on the shelf. They all have similar form but I like the clear bottle, and the emerald color is attractive. It's better looking than Ajax's whisky color.

Retrospective Account

I am very happy with my purchase. My dishes are clean and shiny and my hands feel soft and smooth. I am not afraid to do my dishes before I go out for the evening because my hands look and feel good. It also has a good clean odor. This gives me more confidence that my dishes are clean. I plan on continuing to buy Palmolive unless something better comes out and is less expensive. But it will have to be proven to me.

INTERPRETATION OF CONSUMER PROTOCOL

The consumer's habit of buying Palmolive is not just a blind, automatic response to wanting a washing-up liquid. She is aware of the basis for her preference and remains open to the idea that new brands may come along that could be better. The habitual purchase of Palmolive is to ensure consistency of benefits in terms of effectiveness, cost, intrinsic appeal, social appropriateness, and so on:

Effectiveness

Dishes are made clean and shining.
Even greasy skillets and frying pans are made clean.
Hands are kept soft.
Hands are never itchy after using Palmolive.

Cost

The price of Palmolive is competitive and less expensive than Ivory dishwashing liquid.
Palmolive is economic to use, with only one squirt needed for a full load and with suds lasting for a long time.

Intrinsic Appeal

The packaging of Palmolive is pretty—an emerald green, in a clear plastic container.

Palmolive has a nice clean smell.

Social Appropriateness

Her mother and friends use it.

She can identify with the women in the TV advertisement.

If this consumer is representative of the market segment cultivated by Palmolive, then the firm has done a good job of matching their offering to the segment's choice criteria. Palmolive should continue to ensure that

1. Their brand maintains superiority in effectiveness (cleaning properties and gentleness to hands) as such superiority is a critical advantage.
2. The cost per dishload remains competitive.
3. Advertising appeals stress the product's effectiveness both in cleaning and in the care of hands.
4. Distribution is extensive and out-of-stock positions avoided so that the habitual buying patterns of customers are not broken.

A competitor entering this market would probably have little difficulty in getting those in the segment to try a sample of the product. The problem would be converting customers from Palmolive. For a rival brand to convert from Palmolive, it must be perceived as having greater effectiveness. The other factors (i.e., cost, intrinsic appeal, and social appropriateness) are not as important to the marketing of this product—and would be less likely to effect a conversion.

PICKING

Consumers who have the same life vision may differ in their product wants—or at least have different priorities as to which product wants to satisfy. This is because life goals are underdetermining of what products should be sought: it is beliefs that develop and come to shape how goals are expressed in product wants. Even when beliefs shape the want for a particular product class, the choice criteria may be too general to determine brand preference. In such a situation, consumers may or may not seek additional information to refine their choice criteria enough to determine a brand preference.

The amount of information collected by the consumer depends not on how much information is needed to know everything there is to know about a brand but on how much information is required to determine brand preference. The consumer approach to information gathering seems to be purely pragmatic. Consumers collect and evaluate information only to the point where they can establish a brand preference. A brand preference often becomes clear without the information search needed to make the consumer an expert on the product class.

In relation to the function for which the product is being bought, where the consumer believes that all the brands being considered are equally as good—or at least, not sufficiently different to undertake a further information search—the consumer may resort to just *picking* (Ullmann-Margalit and Morgenbesser, 1977). This situation is analogous to a smoker picking the next cigarette from the pack. Once it is accepted that collecting additional information has a cost, the consumer may rightly believe picking to be justified. The pick itself may be said to be based on a *whim* (i.e., the reasons for brand choice are not apparent) or at *random* (i.e., if reasons guide the consumer, they cannot be characterized.)

Indifference to Brands

Consumer indifference as to which brand to buy does not necessarily mean that the consumer believes the brands are all clones or tokens of each other except for their individual brand names. The consumer may indeed regard the cluster of brands being considered as all equivalent to each other and so be indifferent as to which to choose. However, brands may in fact be perceived as very different in one way or another from each other, but from the consumer's point of view, such differences are perceived as being of no significance to the performance of the functions for which the product is being sought. In this case, the consumer can be said to have a "holistic" want (Schick, 1984). A consumer's want for some class of product is holistic if he or she has no additional want for any specific refinement or particularization of the want. Thus a consumer may have a holistic want for a carton of milk which means he just wants a carton of milk, and does not care about differences among type (e.g., skim, low fat, full fat, and so on) or brands (e.g., Borden, Sealtest, and so on).

Rationalization in Picking Behavior

Promotion has a role to play in catching the pickers and giving them a reason for not just picking by

- Emphasizing differences among brands.
- Emphasizing that these differences do make a difference for the consumer and so are relevant to choice.

Sometimes advertising by just developing familiarity with a brand name may do enough to swing the sale and prevent a picking situation from arising. Many consumers implicitly follow the rule, "In case of doubt as to which of several brands to buy, buy the one that is most familiar."

The incidence of picking behavior is difficult to assess since just asking people will not be revealing. After making a purchase, consumers may rationalize their choice to reduce dissonance. Such rationalizations could turn a picking situation into one where the brand is habitually bought as consumers come to believe their rationalizations.

Picking Low Involvement Products

Pure picking behavior is not too common even when there appears little consumer involvement with the product. On the surface, a product that is of little significance to the consumer is likely to be one where brand choice is more likely to be based on picking. But, even in this situation, many consumers try to avoid picking. They search the package and examine the point of purchase display, brand name, instructions, list of ingredients, and so on, to justify their preference for one brand over another. Hence, if a firm cannot make its brand competitively distinct, it needs to think about how it can distinguish the rest of the offering from rival offerings if picking behavior is likely to be a problem. Brand image or emotional appeals here can be crucial.

Although picking is associated with low involvement products such as gasoline, all picking situations are not related to such products. Picking may occur among brands of a product class that perform a salient function for the consumer (e.g., a detergent). Nonetheless the consumer might strongly believe that all the brands of interest will perform the function satisfactorily. In other words, the consumer may not perceive any differences that are significant to performance. However, many consumers seek to avoid picking even with low involvement products. For some consumers it seems that every brand choice must be justified— a compulsion driven by the possibility of regret if differences among brands prove to have relevance. Choosing wisely is a social norm, and a subsequent discovery that another brand is better is for some consumers tantamount to making an error. However slight the error, it reflects on self-esteem and gives rise to regret that is out of proportion to the importance of the purchase. To some consumers, buying wisely has a satisfaction all of its own regardless of the importance of the purchase. For many consumers there is no liberation from the burden of past buying errors which induces in them an overconcern with avoiding errors in the future.

Relationship Between Picking and Habit

Picking and habit are not unrelated. Consumers may rationalize their choices after picking and such rationalizations may form the basis for habitually buying the brand. Hence, it is important for firms to try and catch the consumer who just picks.

Illustrative Protocol Statement Involving Picking

The following is an extract from a protocol statement that illustrates picking behavior:

> When I was abroad on vacation I found my hairspray was nearly finished. Trying to find the local equivalent of Caryl Richards (the brand I usually buy), I was faced with 16 different brands. I had no idea which to get but managed to narrow the choice to seven which advertised themselves as for "hard to control" hair. They all seemed more or less the same, even down to price, so there was nothing to do but select one at random. Even as I picked it up I knew it would not do the same job as my usual brand—but then I knew that none of the others would either so it didn't really matter which I chose—it would be just a question of making do till I got home.

The consumer narrowed the choice from 16 different brands to just seven brands by deciding to consider only those brands that advertise themselves for "hard-to-control hair." Whatever other differences there were among the brands were not relevant to this consumer's purposes. Hence, she just picked one at random.

A brand that makes no claim to possessing a particular benefit or to possessing an exceptional level of the benefit is likely to be passed over for one that does if that benefit is what the consumer seeks. Brands may be ruled out at the point of sale because they fail to proclaim their critical advantage. In this case, none of the seven brands claiming to be for hard-to-hold hair distinguished themselves in their claims, packaging, or price sufficiently to give the consumer a reason for preferring them. If a firm's brand was one of the seven, it should have provided and proclaimed a sufficiently attractive advantage to act as a reason for preferring the brand. Since this consumer was highly committed to her usual brand, she is unlikely to be constantly experimenting with new hair sprays. A rival brand would have to *promise*—and *provide*—something very special by way of hair control to get the consumer to try the brand, let alone convert to it.

Consumers seek to avoid picking behavior and will try to identify meaningful differences to make their choice of brand more rational. The following protocol statement is illustrative:

> When buying staples I tend to get the same product repeatedly if I am satisfied with it. It saves time, effort, and thought, and avoids the risk of mistakes.
>
> Recently I spent a long vacation abroad and was faced with a large amount of shopping which had to be done quickly. At a big supermarket I soon filled the shopping cart but came to a halt before the shelf containing laundry powders. I searched for my usual "Tide" only to find it wasn't there. I had a momentary sense of almost panic as I scanned the shelves looking at brand names and wondering how to choose. Back home I might have compared prices if my usual brand was unobtainable. Here, even the prices were unfamiliar and I felt I had no basis for my choice. Then the label "Daz" caught my eye. That was it! At least it was a brand I'd heard of even if I'd never used it. The familiarity of the name convinced me I need look no further.

LIKING/INTRINSIC PREFERENCE

There are always reasons for intentional action and there are always reasons for brand preference. This is so even in the case of habit and picking behavior. In the case of habit, consumers act as if they are following an agreed policy to go on buying the same brand to provide a standard solution to a standard problem. Nonetheless, such a policy evolves from the reasons that led to the initial purchases of the brand. In the case of picking, the reasons for preferring a specific brand—as opposed to the reasons for preferring the strategy of picking or for preferring the set of brands from which picking takes place—are so superficial and ephemeral that they may not be identified. However, something, perhaps the position of the brand on the shelf or an eye-catching container, no doubt momentarily operates as a trigger leading to brand choice.

Reasons for brand preference can be intrinsic or extrinsic or a combination of both (Von Wright, 1962). Where brand preference is *intrinsic,* it is based purely on subjective liking: we prefer the brand because we like it best. In the case of *extrinsic preference,* there are objective grounds for the preference. (Extrinsic preference will be dealt with at length later in this book.)

Nature of Intrinsic Preference

An intrinsic preference simply reflects liking. It is reached without the deliberation that goes with decision-making. Even Freud once acknowledged that "there are times when a man craves a cigar simply because he wants a good smoke." When intrinsic preference is the sole criterion for brand preference, there is no further purpose to buying beyond the feelings evoked.

Purchases based purely on intrinsic preference are rational. However, some writers (Knox, 1968) find them "incompletely rational" because the purchase is made purely because it pleases and not for any identifiable objective reason. If consumers were asked to provide reasons for their intrinsic preference, these reasons would simply describe the type of enjoyment expected. The answer would not tell the questioner why the consumer likes what he likes. Thus, someone who is asked why he or she enjoyed a show might answer that it was "exciting" or "thrilling"—words that convey the *form* of enjoyment experienced. Expressions of intrinsic preference refer to the pleasure given:

"The *style* is good looking."
"The *name* just pleases me."
"The *feel* is pleasant."
"The *smell* is fresh."

"The *sound* is relaxing."

"The *taste* is refreshing and I like the flavor and the crispness of the cereal."

"It is the prettiest bottle on the shelf. They all have similar form but I like the clear bottle and the color is attractive."

Some producers go to extreme lengths to signal whatever is likely to convey intrinsic appeal. In some countries the debate goes on about orange trees being injected with compound to make the fruit more orange; about butter being made more yellow by introducing dyes into cow fodder; eggs made brown and yolks more yellow by feeding battery hens with colorants.

The reasons for one person's intrinsic preference are apt to be incomprehensible to those whose tastes are radically different. One consumer may like a particular tie or find his mouth watering at the sight of pecan pie—but the tie and the food may be positively disliked by the next person questioned.

Intrinsic preference can apply to anything associated with the product, so that the brand itself may not be bought purely on its own merits but because of its associations. Thus, there can be an intrinsic preference for shopping at a particular store and the brand may be purchased merely because the store stocks it. Similarly, there are those who get pleasure from receiving goods by mail and may buy a particular brand because it is promoted by mail order.

When advertisers quote intrinsic reasons for preference, their claims are matters of opinion. No claims of false advertising can be involved. Advertisers only get into trouble if they claim "most people" agree with their claims without the support of survey evidence.

Intrinsic Versus Extrinsic Preference

In contrast to intrinsic preference, extrinsic preference is based on reasons that are objectively seen as instrumental in meeting some function, for example,

"The *style* is fashionable."

"The *name* Rolls Royce suggests quality."

"The *feel* is that of expensive leather, which makes people think I'm wealthy."

"The *smell* is strong enough to eliminate tobacco odors."

"The *sound* is loud enough to scare away a thief."

"The *taste* of the mouthwash tells me it is a germ killer."

Intrinsic preferences are likely to be more stable than extrinsic preferences because they are not something that is reasoned about. But intrinsic preferences do change with education and new associations, for example,

"I liked my name until I was told it sounded like a girl's name."

"I liked the style until I was shown how vulgar and ornate it was."

"The feel was pleasant until someone suggested it was the way a snake feels."

"I liked the smell of the fragrance until she started wearing it and this turned me off it."

"I liked the taste until I discovered they were frogs' legs."

"I liked it best until I heard the price was only $15. Then I saw it as less distinguished and attractive."

The distinction between intrinsic and extrinsic preference explains one seeming contradiction between what consumers say and what they actually do. For example, a respondent may claim to prefer Salem cigarettes but may nevertheless buy True cigarettes on a regular basis. The contradication is explained when it is realized that the respondent's *intrinsic* preference is for Salem cigarettes (for he prefers the taste) but his *extrinsic* preference is for True cigarettes (for they contain less tar and nicotine). Choice criteria based on intrinsic preference may take second place to choice criteria based on extrinsic preference as when consumers battle current inclinations in the interests of future fitness. Similarly, an intrinsic preference for butter rather than margarine may be subordinated because of an extrinsic preference for good health.

Purely intrinsic preferences can be a problem to identify. In the first place, consumers find it difficult to verbalize what it is they like about a product. One reason for this is that we do not have a rich vocabulary for expressing different types of pleasure and liking. In the second place, consumers may only seem to choose on the basis of intrinsic preference. For instance, the theatregoer may or may not choose the play most likely to be enjoyed but may consider which play is best for impressing friends. Preferences in beverages and alcoholic drinks are notoriously influenced by product image. Thus, although U.S. beers are becoming more bland and homogeneous in taste (so that in blind-taste tests consumers cannot distinguish between them) beer drinkers still demand some particular brand—the brand with the image with which the drinker can best identify. Expressed likings may simply be prudent, as when someone at a college interview claims to prefer the sound of classial music to rock music.

In any case, both extrinsic and intrinsic preferences usually influence brand choice. Consumers may buy a chocolate bar simply on the ground that they like its taste, but few consumers buy a car regardless of price and other considerations simply because they like the style. Any serious purchase generally involves extrinsic as well as intrinsic preference.

Even in the choice of food there is the question of calories, leading to the current insistence on "liteness"—"lite" beer, "lite" jello, "lite" ice-cream, even "lite" hamburgers and a decline in sales of eggs and butter. Manufacturers are trying to extract the fat, salt, and sugar while leaving the taste the same. Thus, through the use of artificial sweeteners, Americans now consume 50% less sugar than 10 years ago. Interestingly, the more the desire to keep trim affects the intake of candy, the more consumers want to have the best when they do indulge. The current craze for expensive chocolates is one result.

Intrinsic Appeal and Segmentation

Although consumer choices may seldom be based purely on intrinsic preference, intrinsic appeal may nonetheless provide a critical advantage and a basis for segmentation. Flavor segmentation is becoming more common with multi-flavored coffees, teas, vinegars, and mustards.

In the area of aesthetics, intrinsic preference may take second place to the desire for competitive display. As an article in *The Economist* (October 6, 1984) points out, the Japanese have focused more on this than good design:

The Japanese have until very recently concentrated their design effort on the factory floor layout, in order to produce inexpensive, functional but unaesthetic products. For example, the Walkman cassette player is a wonder of miniaturisation, not much else. . . .
    The Japanese manufacturers, however, are quite frank about their objectives: to flatter a young, affluent and spoilt generation that loves to show off. Take a closer look at the effects of minia-

turisation. Japanese firms have put calculators on watches. The proud owner has to squint and use a toothpick to do sums. No ergonomics this. But the product has the serious, I-mean-business, appeal that umpteen pens in a breast pocket cannot provide.

In the field of entertainment, intrinsic appeal can vary with mood (Gosling, 1969), e.g.,

Antipleasure Mood	Entertainment Sought
Nerves feeling jangled	Something soothing
Feeling dull	Something exciting
Feeling bored	Something amusing
Feeling things are unmanageable	Something nostalgic

Culture and Intrinsic Preference

Intrinsic preferences are often idiosyncratic. Many, if not most, such preferences however, are culturally acquired or result from past pleasant associations. Thus, culinary tastes and, less obviously, intrinsic preferences for sounds and smells are generally cultural. But intrinsic aesthetic tastes in particular are educable. People who start looking to justify their intrinsic aesthetic preferences in, say, music or art may find these justifications change their perceptions. This in turn affects how they feel towards the piece of music or the piece of art, which, in turn, may lead to a change in intrinsic aesthetic preferences (Shaper, 1983). Psychologists Zajonc and Markus (1982) discuss the cultural acquisition of food preferences and speculate how preferences (and perhaps attitudes) are acquired and modified. They take examples of food preferences (e.g., chili peppers) that are acquired only after overcoming an initial aversion to the product and show how the introduction of both affective supports (such as parental reinforcement and social conformity pressures) and cognitive supports (such as beliefs about the nutritional qualities of the food) help to gradually overcome the aversion.

Undifferentiated Brands and Picking, Habit, and Intrinsic Preference

In markets saturated with low cost undifferentiated brands, consumers frequently merely choose rather than decide among brands as there is low customer involvement with the product. Advertising agents dealing with these markets were once apt to characterize such consumers as capricious, irrational, conformist, emotional, ignorant, and lazy as a way of voicing their own frustration at being unable to explain consumer behavior. The consumer, in fact, may be acting highly rationally. If a consumer believes that each of the brands he considers will satisfactorily do the job he has in mind, that brand differences are too numerous to investigate and do not matter anyway, then (given these beliefs) he is unlikely to take brand choice seriously. The rules of picking, habit and intrinsic preference may be the best way to proceed when consumers are given no reason to behave otherwise.

Advertisers need to provide consumers with a memorable reason for *both* remembering their brand and selecting it before others. All too often the advertising could apply to any of the brands on the market without the consumer noticing anything wrong. There are two reasons for this. One is the belief that when a product is the most advertised it will be the most remembered—and hence most likely to be chosen in a picking situation. This ignores the quality of the advertising by competitors. The second belief is that it is better to bypass the mind by a purely emotional appeal. The trouble with a purely emotional appeal (like the recent TV campaign suggesting that students without a computer are at a considerable disadvantage at school) is that it frequently does not provide the motivation for buying the particular brand but only for buying the product class.

Illustrative Protocol Statement Involving Intrinsic Preference

The following is an example of a protocol statement where buying was based purely on intrinsic preference:

> I heard a song on FM 93 which had two male vocalists singing with a lovely blending of voices. The next time I heard it I listened more closely. One was American, the other had a foreign accent and I assumed it must be Julio Iglesias, whom I'd heard before. The melody kept haunting me so much that I thought it would be rather nice to have the record but I made no effort to get it. In any case I didn't know the title of the song and regard the buying of pop records as a complete waste of money.
>
> This week I was browsing around the shops and absentmindedly window shopping. As I gazed at records I saw a single entitled "To All the Girls I've Loved Before," sung by Willie Nelson and Julio Iglesias. I knew this was it as the title words are repeated

throughout the song. I went into the store and asked if they had that record on tape. They had but when I looked at the other songs I didn't recognize any of them except "April in Portugal"— because that song is a favorite I decided to get the tape rather than the single disk.

It's very unusual for me to buy a pop record—something I never do. I'm not sure what made me get this one. The words are corny but there is a special quality in the way the voices blend that really appealed to me.

The consumer bought the tape purely because of the enjoyment anticipated to arise from listening to the songs sung by the two singers and not for any objective reasons. This consumer derives some satisfaction from refraining from buying pop records not only because this saves money but because he associates pop records with actually wasting money. However, he does like some pop records and therefore has a passive want for them.

There are many people who, like this consumer, are inhibited from buying pop records because they consider buying such records to be a waste of money. A record has to be a real "hit" with them before they will go out and buy it. Such people need to be shown that pop record buying is endorsed by the people they admire.

SUMMARY

Consumer decision-making involves *deciding-to-buy* a brand as a result of deciding-that it possesses more of the desired attributes than rival brands. Such decision-making contrasts with mere choosing where little or no deliberation occurs because choice is not regarded as problematic. Choices based on decision-making cannot be known in advance of the decision—at least not at the individual level.

Choices based on *habit* are in line with past choices so knowledge of past choices is predictive of future choices. Habitual buying of certain brands saves expense, time and effort, reduces the risk of unpleasant surprises, ensures consistency of benefits and affirms the wisdom of past actions. Habit is not just a blind, automatic response to the recurrence of some want. Consumers remain open to persuasion in generally viewing themselves as open to new ideas.

Choices based on *picking* are based on whim or simply represent random choice. Picking from among brands involves no decision-making or even any conscious choosing of a brand. In picking, consumers are acknowledging that the differences among the brands being considered are of no significance for the performance of the functions for which they are buying the product; that the particular refinements among brands are of no interest. Consumers seek to avoid picking since there is the possibility of regret if differences among brands subsequently turn out to be relevant.

Purchases based exclusively on *intrinsic preference* are purchases based purely on liking. Since only liking is involved, there is no deliberation on objective choice criteria and so no decision-making is involved. Reasons for intrinsic preference refer to the form of pleasure or enjoyment given or anticipated but such reasons will not tell the questioner why the consumer likes what he likes.

IMPLICATIONS FOR MARKETING

1. Where consumer choice is based on *habit,* past choices can be used to predict future choices.

   (a) Where a firm wishes to convert customers from habitually buying a rival brand, the firm's offering or marketing strategy should promise additional benefits to compensate the consumer for undertaking the risk of change, the additional learning and effort involved and the anticipated frustration that results from making an error.

   (b) In seeking to change consumer habits the firm should appeal to the social norm about "giving something new a try" while concentrating on educating the consumer to recognize that a better deal is being offered.

   (c) Where the firm seeks to retain the patronage of its habitual customers, it must focus on building up resistance to brand switching by both reassuring its customers that they are already buying the best while updating/upgrading their offering to preempt competition. Such a strategy is facilitated when a firm has a genuine critical advantage.

2. Where consumers merely pick at random or on the basis of whim which brand to buy, the firm should recognize this as signalling indifference as to differences among the brands being considered.

   (a) Where picking is extensive, firms should modify their offering to provide consumers with some reason to reinforce their natural disposition not to pick but to have a definite preference.

   (b) Where a firm cannot distinguish its product from that of its competitors, it may still catch the pickers by increasing the familiarity of its brand and associating it with an attractive image.

3. Where consumers choose a brand purely on the basis of intrinsic preference, the firm's product must be designed to be most liked by the target customer group.

(a) Where a firm cannot produce a more likeable product than that of competitors, the firm should seek to get the consumer to choose on the basis of additional criteria. Thus the advertisement that claims M & M chocolates "melt in your mouth and not in your hands" is asking the consumer to consider the additional criteria of convenience.

(b) Where a firm cannot educate consumers into changing their tastes, the firm might try to change tastes by associating their brand with the people, items, events, and scenes with which the target audience currently identifies.

5
Rationality in Buying

When consumers are faced with uncertainty as to which product or brand to buy they seek to resolve that uncertainty by evaluating the alternatives. They are engaged in decision-making: the *issue* facing the consumer is a choice from a set of alternatives of which any single one is an *option*. As consumers decide, they resolve the issue by making a choice. In contrast with the last chapter, this is not "mere choice" but rather is a "choice with deciding."

The consumer does not deliberate every purchase; every purchase is not the result of a decision. For consumers to consider the buying occasion to be one for a decision, they must

- Believe that the degree of uncertainty faced and the significance of the purchase warrant deliberation.
- Be prepared and in a position to undertake the task of decision-making.

Neither condition need be present on every buying occasion.

Consumers may make up their minds as to what to buy without reasoning out which is best for them. Such a neglect of reasoning does not in itself signal a lack of rationality. As Pears (1984) says, wants and beliefs have a natural tendency to sort themselves out and to achieve high rationality without explicit reasoning. With habitual buys, brand choice is more or less automatic, with consumers at best reassuring themselves that past precedent constitutes a sufficiently good reason for continuing with the same brand. With picking, consumers are unwilling to evaluate differences among brands to establish the significance of the differences for them. Instead, the consumer simply picks from those offered. Finally, in the case of choice based on intrinsic preference, choice results from immediate liking and nothing else.

It is uncertainty about the costs and benefits attached to individual options that gives rise to the need for a decision. However, the motive for undertaking the effort needed to make a decision may relate more to the anticipation of future regret if an error is made than it does to the anticipation of possible future benefits, as shown in the following extract from the consumer protocol statement in Chapter 3.

> If I choose the wrong sewing machine I am going to feel angry and frustrated for a long time, as a sewing machine should last forever.

Whatever the consumer's initial disposition as to preferences, the deliberation that occurs in decision-making may result in a choice contrary to earlier inclinations. The decision-making process is essentially a learning process, and learning brings fresh insight that can radically change initial beliefs. The process of decision-making is a process of *coming to prefer* what is finally bought. Before that process occurs, that is, before the decision is made, the consumer cannot be said to prefer anything.

DESCRIPTIVE VERSUS PRESCRIPTIVE DECISION-MAKING

There is a vast literature on decision-making. Some of this literature deals with *descriptive* decision-making (i.e., the way decisions are actually made) but most is concerned with *prescriptive* decision-making.

In prescriptive decision-making, rules and rule-based techniques for reaching optimal decisions are laid down. Decision-makers are told how to follow some iterative procedure consisting of

Setting the goal of the decision.
Identifying alternatives.
Identifying the differential consequences of the alternatives.
Evaluating these consequences in terms of goals to reach an optimal decision.

Following such prescriptions cannot, of course, guarantee a good decision, for all real decisions involve uncertainties. Consumer decision-making involves visualizing the consequences of buying one brand instead of another *and* visualizing the future preference for these consequences (March, 1978). If consumers were able to sample all options in the light of future preferences, they might know which was best for them. This is not possible, however, and current choices reflect guesses about future outcomes and preferences.

Some models of consumer decision-making (e.g., the multi-attribute (compensatory) model) use the rational (prescriptive) model for predicting what actually occurs. Consumers, it is assumed, act as if following the rules exemplified by the rules of prescriptive decision-making. We will not review this literature at the present stage except to say that there is no reason to assume a general adherence to any prescriptive model. The process of moving from wants and beliefs to buying preferences is in fact unlikely to follow just one approach since there are many equally plausible inference structures or styles of practical reasoning open to the consumer.

Those with an interest in descriptive decision-making seek to categorize and systematize the various ways people make decisions under various conditions such as information possessed, time pressure, the importance of the purchase and so on. Even prescriptive decision theorists are beginning to recognize the need to know how people actually make decisions if for no other reason than to learn what people are in fact capable of doing. In this chapter, we are concerned with how consumers make decisions or at least the facets of actual decision-making that are of interest to marketing managers.

RATIONALITY IN DECISION-MAKING

Are consumer buying decisions always or ever highly rational? The answer depends on what we mean by rational. On the ground that chosen behavior is voluntary behavior and all voluntary behavior is assumed to be carried out to maximize satisfaction some economists (e.g., Becker, 1976) still hold to the tradition that all chosen behavior is rational. In line with the claim that all chosen behavior is rational, it is argued that all human action makes sense within the context of that person's mental representation of the social world. Most economists, however, introduce some criterion to which behavior must conform if it is to be described as rational. At a minimum, they insist on a transitivity of preferences so that if the consumer prefers A to B and B to C she should also prefer A to C.

Economists view acting rationally as equivalent to proceeding in a logical way to maximize the satisfaction of wants taking into account the intensity of the wants, the probability of the wants being met and the effect of satisfying one want rather than another want. Economists take wants as given. In sharp contrast to the psychoanalytic position, there are no irrational wants on this basis since rationality confines itself to rationality of means for satisfying wants.

Prescriptive quantitative models of decision-making tend to assume a high level of rationality. But quantitative models have difficulty capturing the rationality that takes account of appeals to moral rules, social pressures, and actions performed because we think these things respectable (Kirsh, 1983) though attempts continue to take at least social influences into account (Ajzen and Fishbein, 1980).

Consumers *do* seek to be rational, but the degree to which they are rational varies as basic competences, reasoning styles, and emotional unconscious biases vary. Even when consumers deliberate in a highly rational manner given their beliefs, they may not appear very rational to those not sharing those beliefs. In fact, we still have a lot to learn about how consumers weight costs and benefits, reconcile opposed reasons for different choices, and so on. Although we know that the decision fixes the relative weights attached to reasons we are only recently getting some understanding of how consumers discount benefits according to the uncertainty of getting them or according to their remoteness in time.

In deciding among brands, consumers carry out mental experiments by manipulating symbolic forms to help visualize the consequences of buying while relating such consequences to present or future wants. Sometimes, as with the adoption of some new fashion, such mental experiments may be in the nature of role-playing to anticipate the pleasure and the reaction of others if the item is bought and worn. Choices based on this process may fall short of expectations because of errors arising from lack of information, mistakes in reasoning, or emotional biases that distort weightings of costs and benefits. Less obviously, when buying a product for the first time, buyers are often unsure what they want, how they will like the product, or what they will want after they obtain what they thought they wanted.

Here, we will view rationality as a matter of degree ranging from the highly rational to the irrational, bearing in mind that rationality does not guarantee correct choices (which also depend on the quality of information possessed). The extent to which consumers decide wisely as well as correctly depends on

1. The rationality of the want itself, since it could be argued that not all wants are rational.
2. Whether the products or brands being considered include the best buy for the consumer.
3. Whether the consumer correctly perceives the relevant facts about options.
4. The degree to which the consumer rationally processes information.

Whenever such information is incorrectly processed, it may be termed a manifestation of irrationality (Pears, 1984). This may be much too sweeping a judgment, however, since illogical thinking cannot always be equated with irrational thinking. Irrationality carries with it the notion of holding onto wants and beliefs that are contrary to the overwhelming body of evidence showing the harmfulness of the wants or the falsity of the beliefs. A person may be illogical, however, not because he ignores the evidence but because he violates some rule of logical deduction—a frequent occurrence that most of us would hesitate to label irrational behavior. Similarly, it seems wrong to speak of consumers being irrational when we simply mean that their actions are unintelligble or uninformed. As long as consumers intend to act rationally and evaluate objectively to choose what is best for them or those close to them, they are acting rationally, even if their arguments or actions violate logical norms. However, we do accept that consumers can possess irrational wants and irrational beliefs and make biased judgments. (See Figure 7.)

Rationality of Wants

Wants can be irrational. For example, a consumer may want a particular product he or she knows will be injurious without compensating reason (Culver and Gert, 1982). The expression "without there being any compensating reason" is important since consumers may have a justification for seeking injury just as I might agree to surgery to stop the spread of cancer. Thus, some cigarette smokers continue the practice though they acknowledge it is injurious, but claim the risks are compensated by the relief from tension provided by cigarettes.

Government legislators must consider the rationality and irrationality of wants when they are drafting new laws. For example,

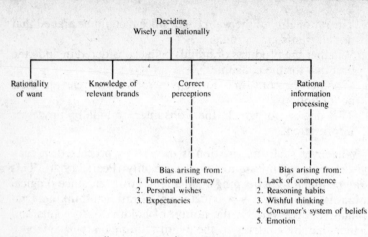

Figure 7 Factors Affecting Rationality in Buying

if drugs (an irrational want) were made legal, it might "unravel the very fabric of society."

With the exception of buying to injure oneself without compensating reason, all consumer wants can be viewed as rational. However, the priority with which wants are satisfied can be debated. Consumers are often both unsure of their priorities and uncertain as to the best specification of what they want. Yet, if this specification is fuzzy, the confidence with which consumers evaluate the costs and benefits attached to the options will also be vague. Whatever confidence consumers seem to exhibit when filling out questionnaires asking them to weight product attributes for relative importance, does not guarantee that the resulting set of weights will be useful or in line with buying behavior. Attribute weightings are never meaningful when respondents are either still open to persuasion as to what they seek or cannot visualize what different sets of weights mean in terms of different configurations of benefits.

When consumers experience doubt in knowing precisely what they want, they also have problems in knowing how much of some attribute they want (e.g., horse power) and in making tradeoffs (e.g., between horse power and fuel economy). There is the additional difficulty of gauging how much of the attribute (e.g., fashion/status) is being provided by each brand. In such situations, consumers do not compare brands on an individual attribute basis but compare the different *configurations* of individual brand benefits. Brand attributes are implicitly weighted in this process for they affect the overall valuation of the brand's configuration of benefits—but this is different than ranking the individual brand's attributes as a basis for ranking the brands themselves.

There is a recognition of the limitations of evaluation in advance of actually consuming or using the product. Evaluation in advance of experience with the product must rely on judgment in selecting the relevant attributes and interpreting the signs of benefits and costs correctly. The consumer is obliged to follow a "coherence theory of truth" (i.e., coherence with what is already known) rather than a "correspondence theory of truth" (i.e., correspondence with the facts stemming from using the product). Hence, the importance of trial and sampling for consumer confidence.

Knowledge of Relevant Alternatives

Using prescriptive decision-making, all the relevant options are a given. But consumers rarely have knowledge of all the products or brands that might be satisfactory. Even if all options could be identified by visits to a number of stores, the consumer may not be prepared to put in the time and effort required.

The extent to which the consumer searches for relevant options depends not only on the risk associated with the purchase and existing knowledge of what is available, but also on beliefs about likely differences among options. If it is believed that the available options are very similar, then extensive search will not be undertaken and those considered will be the ones at hand. A belief that the available options are similar may have arisen before the consumer had actively sought information about a product bought for the first time. This is because the consumer may have passively absorbed many beliefs about the product prior to any thought about buying it. Where the consumer has a predisposition or belief that the relevant options are very different, there will be no need for detailed and extensive search, since a crude mental screening will determine the subset that is in line with wants. It is the brands on the market that are believed to possess differences that are meaningful to the consumer (yet require to be evaluated) that the consumer seeks to identify. Whether this subset includes the best buy for the consumer cannot be guaranteed, since beliefs about options can be erroneous.

Correct Perceptions of the Facts

What consumers might choose under full knowledge of conditions and what they actually choose may diverge somewhat because of wrong beliefs. One source of false beliefs is the misperception of facts leading to false inputs to the mind about brand options. Consumers may misperceive communications on a product or brand because

- They lack the basic skills needed to understand the facts correctly.
- They are predisposed to believe only what is in line with some personal wish.
- Past expectancies bias their perceptions as to what is relevant.

Potential Sources of Bias: Functional Illiteracy

Let us now examine each of these potential sources of bias.

A great many communications about products and brands assume a certain level of literacy, but a fair proportion of the population are functionally illiterate and written communications are either ignored or misread. Even friends are often unaware of the problem. If functional literacy is necessary to understand differences among brands or to distinguish the new from the old in terms of benefits offered, then understanding may not be forthcoming for many consumers. It is often embarrassing for consumers to ask others for this type of help since it exposes their deficiencies while not guaranteeing their understanding. It would be interesting to know how many people who are slow to adopt anything new and who stick to old habits do so for no better reason than that they are unable to understand communications on packages, in advertising, or from salesmen.

Potential Sources of Bias: Personal Wishes

Of more psychological interest are the misperceptions that arise to fit wishes. This is not to suggest that people can see black as white just because this is their wish, but wishes can bias perceptions and create illusions. This is often true regarding the effects of beauty products: instead of real differences, consumers see illusions fostered by the wish for self-improvement. Similarly, consumers can discount information (e.g., such as the harmful effects of drugs) if it does not coincide with their wishes.

When information is discounted, it is just dismissed and not absorbed to allow evaluation. People generally have a problem in facing up to reality if that reality is threatening. But not facing the truth can lead consumers into playing a role or living a lifestyle to feed the illusion or fantasy. This occurs, for example, with groups like motorcycle gangs and punk rock groups.

Potential Sources of Bias: Expectancies

Perceptions are also biased by expectancies. All observation is selective, so we perceive only a small part of what is totally perceptible. What we select depends not only on the intensity, novelty, and complexity of whatever impinges on the senses, but also on what we have come to expect or been taught to look for given our purposes.

Such selectivity may be of the wrong types, however, so that signficant differences between rival offerings are ignored. Products or brands that come to be associated with a certain specific function may tend not be used for other functions for which they are equally suited. An unlikely example was ginger ale, which became so associated with its use as a mixer that for a long time consumers did not consider it as a soft drink.

Rationality in Information Processing

Assuming the consumer's want is not irrational and information about the relevant brand options is correctly received, then the rationality of the decision depends on how correctly the information is processed. When buying, consumers seek to maximize reward after the subtraction of costs. In line with this, consumers want to process information correctly to reach valid conclusions (i.e., beliefs). Hence, the fact that consumers often do not process information correctly needs to be explained (Pears, 1984). Incorrect processing might arise through

- Individual lack of competence
- Certain common (faulty) habits of reasoning
- Wishful thinking
- Consumer's system of beliefs
- Emotion

The above sources of bias are not exhaustive. For a comprehensive listing see Hogarth and Makridakis (1981).

Potential Bias in Information Processing: Lack of Competence

Beliefs may not adjust to the evidence because the consumer lacks the competence to make the adjustment. Individuals vary in their competence to assimilate, analyze, synthesize, and make correct deductions from "facts" collected on products and brands. Neither legislators nor manufacturers can guarantee that inculcating certain facts will lead the consumer to reach the logical conclusion via the rules of valid inference. Consumers are capable of all types of processing errors and fallacies of reasoning.

Potential Bias in Information Processing: Reasoning Habits

Some faulty habits of reasoning are well-documented, such as cognitive psychology's attribution theory. For example, consumers may reach a quick initial judgment about products and brands and are often inclined to hang on to this initial judgment against the evidence either through filtering out contrary evidence or interpreting the evidence to fit.

Additional information is interpreted simply as further confirmation of the initial judgment. Once initial beliefs are formed, they can be difficult to dislodge when bias preselects the information received and determines how it is construed. Consumers often consult their intuitions to arrive at an initial judgment with all subsequent information being viewed as support. Thus, consumers may continue to use sleeping pills because their initial effectiveness induces a belief in them that persists in the face of objective evidence as to their ineffectiveness when used continuously. Again, evidence that stands out is apt to be given much more weight than is justified. Thus, size is often overweighted when value for money is being judged. Advertisers often have to counteract these perceptions by pointing out that their brand of liquid detergent, their brand of shampoo, and so on, is more concentrated and goes much further than rival brands in bigger containers. In general, however, bad reasoning can be exposed and, as Pears says, "cold illusions have no residual force once unmasked."

There are those in marketing who exploit known tendencies of consumers to misconstrue the facts or situation when presented in a certain way. Until the law intervened, some big city retailers had permanent signs outside their stores declaring they were going out of business—and implying that there were bargains inside the store. A more subtle variation of this is advertising that makes such claims as "Brand X gets clothes cleaner" without specifying cleaner than what.

Potential Bias in Information Processing: Wishful Thinking

Wishful thinking is another way in which rationality can be undermined. Consumers subject to wishful thinking have a strong self-interest for something to be true (e.g., to be eternally young) so that uncomfortable beliefs (e.g., that there are no products that will eliminate wrinkles) are resisted. Advertising can reinforce the fantasy and the daydream when it seems people want to believe they can have it all—that upward mobility is ensured by a clean shave; that academic failure can be averted by use of a personal computer; that threats to health can be avoided by scientific advance; and so on. Irrational beliefs can result from wishful thinking if such beliefs arise through the deliberate suppression of evidence that the belief is wrong. Culver and Gert (1982) claim a belief is irrational if

It is held by someone with sufficient knowledge and intelligence to know it is false.

It is contrary to the overwhelming evidence available to the person.

Its contradiction by the evidence is obvious to everyone with similar knowledge and intelligence.

Consumers who want to believe may bias their deliberations and manipulate the evidence to exaggerate the pros and minimize the cons. Holding onto some false belief can be an end in itself when it gives rise to exhilarating, pleasurable effects with reality and fantasy becoming blurred. It was Revson of Revlon who was reputed to have said, "In the factory we manufacture cosmetics, but in the drugstore we sell hope."

Reason can lead consumers to beliefs (e.g., that they have been cheated) that initiate and sustain some emotion (e.g., anger). However, once strong emotions are aroused, the consumer may be unable or unwilling to question or rethink the belief when the belief and the corresponding emotion have come to mutually support each other (Dilman, 1981).

The Consumer's System of Beliefs

Any belief about a product is usually part of a system of beliefs. A strong attack on the one belief calls the rest to mind in its defense. When the medical profession pointed out the greater likelihood of cigarette smokers dying from lung cancer, a whole host of counterarguments were marshalled in defense based on beliefs such as:

"Doctors are often wrong."
"My father smoked four packs a day and lived to be 90."

Even where consumers are seemingly influenced by an initial strong attack on one of their existing beliefs, the undermining of defenses may only be temporary. As they absorb the impact they reconstruct new defenses.

The seller must know the whole system of beliefs that holds back buying. Take the current market for automobiles. Even if the cars coming from Detroit are equal in every respect to the best of foreign cars, there will be no immediate swing back to buying American cars because many consumers doubt or disbelieve the claim that the quality of U.S. cars is on par with foreign cars:

> We decided right off that we wanted a foreign car because they seemed to be made well and I liked their style and design. I had had a BMW before, which had 100,000 miles on it, and I had had no problems. I have friends who have had American cars with 50,000 on their cars and had needed major repairs. There also seemed to be better safety factors with foreign cars. *Consumer Reports* gave the foreign models better reviews. I like Japanese and German cars and these have been consistently rated high by friends and magazines. These cars do not break down as much, thus requiring less maintenance. To me, there is just a world of difference between American and foreign cars.

Since consumer beliefs are the principal determinant of what make of car is bought and beliefs change slowly, the shift in demand is likely to proceed slowly. Detroit must again earn its spurs. Thus, the belief that U.S. cars are poor in quality rests on beliefs such as:

U.S. car workers are not as quality minded as the Germans or the Japanese.
U.S. car advertising has always been full of promise but the product consistently low on quality.

Until the evidence is there about Detroit quality, it is better to stick to what you know are reliable makes.

Until the U.S. car firms identify and disprove the typical *cluster* of beliefs holding back consumer buying, many consumers will continue to rule them out when buying a car. Car makers also need to know precisely how consumers establish high reliability so they can provide the right signals. The technical indicators of quality used by the manufacturer may only partially overlap with the indicators used by the consumer to gauge quality.

Pears (1984) stresses how wishful thinking often supports beliefs that make it easier to yield to temptation. There are still those who deny the connection between smoking and lung cancer, or between drugs and the evils which most of us accept as the inevitable accompaniment of their use.

Perhaps the popularity of Freudian psychology among the public lies in the fact that his theories made it easier to indulge in old and favorite vices. Guilt at indulgence can be a powerful inhibitor to buying. In general, advertisers who effectively remove even trivial guilt ("Go on, treat yourself, you deserve it") will find a receptive audience.

Emotion and Bias

Wishful thinking can have a strong emotional base. In extreme cases, reason cannot function when at the mercy of emotion. An emotional reaction occurs whenever there is a strong negative or positive evaluation of the buying situation sufficient to give rise to a physiological reaction whether directly felt (e.g., excitement) or not (e.g., a rise in blood pressure). We should distinguish the concept of emotion from social reasons that enter into the consumption process, such as when the consumer dispassionately takes account of convention, fashion, or morality in choosing a swimsuit.

Solomon (1980, 1984) views emotions as urgent judgments about one's situation and emotional responses as a species of emergency behavior. He claims that emotions can be purposive and intentionally chosen. For example, a customer may choose to get angry (and not just feign anger) to impress the seller in the hope of getting immediate redress. Solomon argues that emotions (e.g., anger at being cheated) change as beliefs change (e.g., discovering no cheating occurred) and so are not irrational. The fact that emotional responses can be counterproductive occurs because

1. Emotional responses usually occur in situations where expectations, plans, and intentions are upset. As a consequence, spur of the moment judgment substitutes for the rules that would normally be followed.
2. Emotional responses are more in line with short-run rather than long-run interests.

Whenever people are confronted with situations or symbols that represent or signal some extreme contrast in the human condition, an emotional reaction commonly occurs. We are drawn to dramatic portrayals of the preferred life vision and repelled by anything that dramatically threatens its attainment. Hence, advertising commonly associates the brand advertised with the good life or suggests the product is a way of warding off certain threats to the achievement of the good life.

If emotional responses are rational, we would expect such responses to be in line with beliefs. Yet people can be afraid of something (e.g., a mouse) that they know they have no reason to fear (Calhoun 1984). It seems we can reject some beliefs at the intellectual level (e.g., cancer cures and rejuvenation pills), but may still buy the product because other beliefs (e.g., old superstitions or old beliefs) come to the surface to support the purchase. Even in nonextreme cases, emotions channel attention on a limited number of cues and so bias evaluation. If faulty thinking collapses as soon as it is detected and exposed, emotional wishful thinking is more persistent since "consciousness will not put an end to the power of a wish to fascinate and delude."

Logical Principles and Consumer Buying

In markets where brands are numerous and differences among them lack significance for the consumer, brand choice is unlikely to be taken very seriously. It is not surprising that advertising agencies specializing in such markets might come to believe that a good deal of buying is just based on emotional impulse. Even in the 1920s it was argued that advertisers should short-circuit the mind through appeals to the emotions on the ground that appeals to reason are apt to stimulate counterargument in the mind of the consumer (Poffenberger, 1925).

Some cognitive psychologists have taken a particular interest in the way logical principles are violated in making decisions. The work of Kahneman and Tversky (1982) compared the rationality of consumers with the rational rules of expected utility theory. For example, the principle of invariance asserts that two versions of a choice problem that are recognizably equivalent when shown together should elicit the same preference when shown separately. Investigation shows this rule is not generally followed. Students were asked to imagine they had decided to see a play and had bought a $10 ticket but that on entering the theater they discovered they had lost the ticket. Most people, when asked, would not pay another $10 for another ticket. However, if the ticket was not purchased in advance but on entering the theater people find they have lost $10, the situation is different. Most people claim they would go ahead and still pay $10 to see the play. The difference in response was interpreted as arising because of the "topical" organization of mental accounts, that is, each transaction is considered a separate topic and treated separately. The loss of the $10 in cash is entered into an account distinct from that of the play. In contrast, the lost ticket is posted to the account of the play and the unexpected doubling of the cost of the play is difficult to accept. Those interested in such research might consult a recent collection of essays edited by Kahneman, Slovic, and Tversky (1982) and a critical review of the work by Levi (1985). It is now generally accepted that people do evaluate gains differently from losses. However, there is perhaps an additional explanation for this.

Exchange theorists (e.g., Webster, 1975) in social psychology often point out that the rules of economic exchange are carried over into the social sphere. But, more often, the reverse is true. Humphrey (1983) points out that social exchange came before economic exchange and its rules remain dominant. Surely the rule "not to let someone take advantage of you" was a social rule before being a rule of economic exchange? Before children learn to shop they learn to exchange feelings, sentiments, information, and beliefs with others. In social exchanges we are particularly concerned about losing out, saving face, not being made a fool of, and so on. These are important social goals associated with preserving our self-image and signalling to others a competent self.

I believe the rules developed in social transactions operate in consumer buying behavior and that adherence to the rules sometimes conflicts with the rules of rationality as developed by decision theorists. Thus, it could be argued that in violating rational rules in the Kahneman and Tversky experiment the players were adhering to the rules developed for social exchange. Quite simply, consumers hate to pay the other fellow twice for the same service as this violates the rule of fairness governing all types of reciprocity. In order to avoid this siuation it would be predicted that people would probably spend more time looking for the lost ticket than the lost $10.

The results of related experiments by Kahneman and Tversky (1982) can be interpreted similarly. Thus, consumers who have paid a tennis club membership fee will continue to use the club even though tennis elbow makes playing painful. This is perhaps because consumers, as in social exchange, do not want to lose out to those to whom they are in no way obligated. In another of their experiments, consumers seemed no more willing to exert any more effort to save $15 on a $150 purchase than to save $5 on a $50 purchase. An interpretation consistent with the rules of social exchange is that consumers seek to avoid the sense of loss and regret that results from knowing there was even one social encounter where they might have done better. Transactions may be considered individually because they are perceived as social encounters which are always treated as distinct episodes. It is somewhat reminiscent of the Woody Allen character complaining about the restaurant: "The food is horrible and, what's worse, they serve such small portions." Evidently, even when we pay for poor food, we try to get our money's worth by eating all of it.

STUDYING CONSUMER DECISION-MAKING

We can study the consumer's decision-making process through the protocols as described earlier. At each stage, the consumers' actions can be explained in terms of their reasons—that is, what they are trying to accomplish (goals and wants) and their beliefs about the best means of getting there. Once we know these reasons, we can go on to identify the rules being followed. Knowing the reasons and rules is usually enough for understanding individual buying decisions—it is usually more relevant than either an objective specification of buying conditions, the consumer's personality, or whatever is defined as making up the situation or circumstance guiding the consumer. Marketers are interested in how consumers themselves perceive the situation. As we have seen, the situation on which the consumer decides to act is not necessarily the one that matches reality, but is the one that is conceived by the consumer's thought processes. Knowing the objective facts about a situation may not be illuminating when consumers believe their situation to be otherwise. Nonetheless, knowledge of the informational episodes (i.e., when the relevant information is received) can be valuable since the inputs on which perception and thought work come from these episodes.

We need to build up knowledge of our actual or potential customers from facts about individuals. Of course, overall descriptions of consumers in a market need not be confined to summations of individual protocol statements. Just as the description of a forest can be something more than a description of the various types of trees, overall descriptions of consumers need not be restricted to just classifying consumers on the basis of their wants and beliefs. However, it can be argued that knowledge of goals, wants, beliefs, and rules constitute the rock-bottom explanation of consumer buying actions for marketing purposes.

Of particular importance in the following chapters is a specification of the auxiliary reasons or choice criteria used by buyers. Consumer preferences stem from such criteria. As far as extrinsic preference is concerned, the claim is made that, choice criteria in buying can be decomposed into the following five criteria of rationality (Diesing, 1962):

1. Technical criteria such as the performance characteristics of the product.
2. Legalistic criteria such as the law obliging car owners to buy seatbelts.
3. Economic criteria such as price.
4. Integrative criteria such as following convention to ensure that the buyer's purchase helps integrate the consumer either socially or with self.
5. Adaptive criteria such as following advice to help the consumer cope with the anxieties arising from having to adapt to uncertainty and information overload.

There is perhaps a tendency for firms to assess consumer attitudes primarily on technical and economic aspects of their offering and to base their predictions of likely success on this assessment. But technical and economic criteria may be no more significant in determining brand choice than any of the other criteria. Knowledge of the buyer's actual choice criteria is fundamental, but the recognition of potential choice criteria is also important since it can amount to the recognition of a latent want. However, knowledge of actual and potential choice criteria may not be enough to predict likely preferences. We may also need to know how the consumer infers that such criteria are present and what physical or other cues lead the consumer to infer the presence or absences of the sought-after qualities or attributes.

SUMMARY

If there is uncertainty about the costs and benefits attached to various options and the consumer is prepared and in a position to evaluate the options, then brand choice will result from decision-making. The decision process is essentially a learning process that may radically change initial predispositions and beliefs. After identifying brand options, consumer decision-making involves visualizing the consequences or effects of buying one brand instead of another and visualizing future preferences for these consequences.

The extent to which consumers search to identify the alternatives available depends not just on the risk associated with the purchase but also on what knowledge consumers believe they already possess about various brands and their perceptions of the differences among them. Consumers tend to seek out rival brands only to the extent they believe the brands possess meaningful differences.

Consumers often get the facts wrong about a product or brand due to bias arising from

- Functional illiteracy or some other basic skill deficiency, such as poor eyesight
- Personal wishes
- Experience that has taught the consumer certain expectations

Consumers are not equally rational in the way they process information. Processing errors can be due to:

- The individual's lack of competence in reasoning
- General habits of reasoning that are faulty among consumers at large
- Wishful thinking based on strong self-interest leading to the suppression of unpleasant beliefs and the manipulation of evidence
- Consumers' system of beliefs
- Emotion

IMPLICATIONS FOR MARKETING

1. If marketing strategy is to influence the outcome of a buying decision, the firm should first identify buying that involves true decision-making, namely those situations where buyers of the product are consciously aware of their lack of knowledge about the costs and benefits attached to rival brands.

2. In situations where the consumer is uncertain as to the costs and benefits attached to the various brand options, the firm can influence the outcome of the buying decision by signaling in various ways.
   (a) Why is the firm's brand likely to fit what is wanted better than rival brands?
   (b) What benefits are offered and in what amounts over and above rival offerings?
   (c) What costs will be incurred and why these are a better investment than those costs associated with rival brands?
   (d) How can the consumer trust the firm's brand to minimize the possibility of error?

3. If the firm's brand is to enter into the set of brands being considered by the consumer, it should be perceived as having meaningful differences that distinguish it from rival brands. Otherwise, the consumer may consider other brands equivalent.

4. Marketing strategy needs to take into account the distortions and biases that result from a lack of perfect rationality, including
   (a) The possibility of distortions in receiving information due to functional illiteracy, expectations, and wishful thinking.
   (b) The possibility of bias in the processing of information due to lack of competence, faulty reasoning habits, wishful thinking, the consumer's system of beliefs, or emotion.

5. Marketing strategy needs to consider how consumers themselves conceive the situation. Their views may be out of line with what the objective or situational factors would suggest.

6

Grounds for Deciding: Technical and Legalistic Criteria

Before reading this discussion of technical and legalistic criteria for decision-making, the reader should examine the following protocol statement concerned with the purchase of a steam iron. This is a long protocol intended to illustrate the amount and richness of material available from verbal protocols of entire shopping episodes. The reader should try and identify the consumer's goals, wants, beliefs, and choice criteria and think about the implications of these for marketing management.

Readers might choose to rethink their analyses on the basis of the contents of this and subsequent chapters concerned with the other aspects of decision-making. In any case, an analysis of the protocol is given in Appendix A at the end of the chapter.

Illustrative Protocol Statement on the Buying of a Vapor Simac Steam Iron

Anticipatory Account

Well, I'm thinking of buying an iron. It's different from other irons in that it's advertised as a professional iron. When I worked in the [dress design] industry we used a professional iron. Basically I need it because the iron I have at home doesn't work anymore.

I think I don't know a lot about irons. I've never shopped for any iron before. But, I'm not unknowledgeable about irons. My knowledge comes from my use of them [professional irons] in school, in industry, and, in a brochure that sells professional dressmaking equipment, I read a little bit about one of them; it's pretty much what I could tell is exactly what I had used in school and when I was working. It was, with this particular company, about $250, give or take $10.

The only reason that I have a specific iron in mind now is because I saw it advertised. I didn't know that I could purchase a professional-working iron in a retail store like Macy's. They [Macy's] advertised it; I saw it. I said, well, that's something like what I want. I [had] wanted to buy the true professional iron, but the sale price for this one is $100. I'm *hoping* that it is still on sale. But even if it's not on sale, I'll probably buy it because I need a new iron. If it's any more than $150—which I doubt it's going to be—I would probably not— well, *maybe* not purchase it and spend the extra hundred and buy the super professional iron. But I want to see [it], to actually see what it offers, what it does, how it looks, how it feels. But I don't think it's going to be any more than $150.

Before [the advertisement] I hadn't planned on buying one [the mid-priced model]. I *had* planned on buying the professional one for $250 but *that* I had to save up a little bit more for. In all fairness, I would have probably bought that [$250] one.

I don't know anybody else with a professional iron. Nobody else as far as a friend of mine or a relative. Business, yes. But not the medium-priced one. I'd never even heard of it before. Only the professional model or the conventional model.

There's just the one medium-priced brand that I know about, the one on sale. But I really won't know about any other professional-type irons until I go and look. Then I'll know. To tell you the truth, I can't remember the name of the brand. The advertising that Macy's did was in a circular they put in with the Sunday newspaper. It was, I guess, the housewares page. They had a variety of I suppose different houseware items. In the bottom they had I guess maybe three different irons that they offered on sale. And normally I'm not in the habit of looking at such domestic things, but I don't know why I did, but it caught my eye. This particular one. And I said, well, this is a good price as far as what I knew from the other iron and I really do need one because the one I have is working very erratically. I can never depend on it.

The advantage of it [the professional iron] is, it does a better job. With my home iron, sometimes I'll get steam, sometimes I won't. It seems like it's very temperamental. I think—I'm *hoping,* I've never purchased one like this before—that this will be a little bit better. I'm hoping it will be more reliable. I'm thinking for the price difference it *should* be. I think for a conventional iron you can get it for anywhere from like $35, I guess, to $55. This [one] is $100 on sale, so if I'm going on price, for that amount of money it better offer more than a $35 iron. I expect that it would offer more and that it will. And again, it's $150 less than the *professional* professional iron that I was looking at, so I think it's sort of a good compromise. I'm happy with the compromise in between the two.

They [the true professional irons] aren't big. As a matter of fact, they're lighter weight. But the water is held in a separate tank. It's filtered. The water is distilled. And the water is fed through a tube into the iron. It works that way. This [mid-priced model] is very similar in that it has, I think, a little stand, which you fill the water in through. The water is distilled, so it's better for ironing your clothes. You don't get the little water spots from all the minerals. And, they work a little bit better. Well, the ones that I've used have worked a lot better. You can press clothes with greater ease. You don't have the water contained within the iron itself. The water is in a separate area and it's fed through a hose into this iron when you want steam. You could use distilled water with a conventional iron but that's very inconvenient. You have to go out and buy distilled water and keep it separate just to use for your iron. You can use just tap water in one of these.

That [the water] is important but it's not most important. It's how the product performs in getting out wrinkles. And if it does it nice and easy and I'm down there [ironing] for five minutes instead of 15 minutes, that's great. And you don't have to press as hard. I don't believe you do. You don't have to keep going over it. From my use of a professional iron, my past use, it went a lot easier. It seemed to get out wrinkles better. I have used a professional iron in school and in the [fashion] industry. It was just lighter and you didn't have to go over it [the clothes] as many times for it to come out. You pressed the steam, and the steam came out beautifully. No problems. It'll get out wrinkles with greater ease. Maybe now I have to go over it [my clothes] five times. With this, if I have to go over it once, that's great. If I have to spend a little bit more money [it's worth it] to have something that looks a little bit better at the end result. If I press something and it looks fabulous. I don't want it to look like I've sat at home and *over*pressed the garment, and you wear it out, it looks terrible. But if I do something very easy, it looks professionally done—that's very important to me. [With other irons] it's possible to be overpressed. It'll look like you overworked the garment. It'll get soiled; it'll get mashed down. Through school we learned this. We would get a lesser grade if the garment was overpressed, what we'd call overworked. It's not, maybe not, say, the back or the sides. It might be a collar that you've spent overpressing and maybe you fold it down and you press a sharp crease into it, which collars shouldn't have, a sharp crease. People do that. It happens. They think they're being thorough but they're doing it wrong.

Contemporaneous Account

[Subject sees the display models and immediately recognizes the one she is interested in, a Simac model. She lifts up the iron.] Oh, I didn't realize it had this—the feature that you can lay the iron down on this—I don't know what you call it—this pad. I like that a lot! It might be safer, too. It won't fall over. If you hit the ironing board it won't fall over.

I'm not crazy about the looks but I don't care. It doesn't matter to me. Nobody's going to—I'm not going to be doing this [ironing] when we have company or anything, so I really don't care.

It's a little heavier than I thought it would be. I would say it's about the same [weight] as the one I use now. The only thing I don't like is where if you had just the individual iron you could rest it on the board. I would have to find a place for this [reservoir and pad]. I guess I could put it toward the end of the ironing board, but then it takes up room on the ironing board.

[Examining the box.] Oh, look, they give you a toll free number for any problems. That's nice to know. And I could return it to Macy's within, I guess, a certain amount of time if I don't like it—if I'm not happy with its performance.

I don't see if it's still on sale. I don't know. Let me check and see. [Looks at price tag. The price has been marked down.] It's still on sale. Generally they'll [Macy's] have it [announced with a sign] in red, you know, "On Sale."

[Twisting knob.] I want to see how the knob moves, if it's easy. You know, if I'm not going to break a fingernail on it or not. The things like that which are important to me. I just want to see the different settings it has. [She checks. It has settings for linens, cottons, wool, silk, and synthetics.] It has all the settings that I would need. It tells you right there. It tells you where the steam comes in, which is great, but most irons do that anyway.

[She looks at the bottom of the iron.] It doesn't have very many steam vents. [She hesitates.] I suppose these [fewer vents] will work greater. [Pauses.] They should work better if there's fewer of them. Well, it's a steam iron, OK, with continuous steaming. It's advertised as a professional iron system: water reservoir, continuous steam, so. . . . [She looks at the next model on display, a Sunbeam iron.] I don't like this [Sunbeam] because it's mostly plastic. It feels very light. This is a Sunbeam on sale for $32. It's just a conventional iron. It has your different settings: steam, permanent press. [Checks bottom of Sunbeam to compare number of steam vents.] It has more steam vents but maybe they don't work as well as the one with fewer steam vents. It just feels. . . . [She lifts the Simac model again.] This *does* feel a bit more substantial. I suppose with an iron you do need the weight. I mean, I don't want to put it on the stove to heat it up, you know.

[Again looking at the Simac model.] This seems like a very short cord, though, shorter than mine. [She checks the cords. There are two cords coming from under the pad, one slightly larger in diameter than the other. [I don't think it gets any longer. Oh, it does? [She pulls one cord out about an inch.] Oh, fabulous! [She refers to one cord and then the other.] Hey, you know what, it probably goes— this probably winds in there and it comes out there, so it *is* a long cord. So you can adjust the cord, which is really nice! So then you don't have a lot of loose cord lying around. It [the loose cord] gets caught up in the machine. I'm sure that's what it does. [She checks more closely.] No, I'm not sure, because this [cord] has to be thicker, this has to have the water coming through. Yes, it is thicker. Do you see the two wires? Well, let's take a look. [She refers to the box.] No, it doesn't say here. I don't like that. I like it when they list all the features on the box, because then you know what you're getting. [Here] they just give the addresses: addresses, telephone numbers. It's a machine, they should have a little more.

That's interesting. [Points to "Made in Italy" on the box.] Look at that. Doesn't make any difference, though. Not at all. Not in the least! I just care about how it works. That's all I care about. The only

thing I know about the company is that they make food processing
products [like] pasta makers, ice cream makers.

So I'm going to get it and try it. And we'll see how it works. And if it
doesn't work how I like, I'll bring it back. Macy's has a very good
return policy. It's never a problem returning anything at Macy's.

Retrospective Account

I think I'll keep it. The only reason maybe I won't keep it is when I
first used it I didn't know exactly how to adjust the steam cycle. I
had it adjusted at one point and it not only gave steam but it gave
water drops on the garment too, which I didn't like, but I'm thinking
maybe just because it was new, getting the water first from the tank
to the iron might have caused that, and not having this adjusted
properly. [She refers to the steam selector knob.] I adjusted it and it
seemed to work a little bit better. The only thing I was confused with
in the instruction booklet was, the direction to turn this [steam
selector knob] wasn't very clear so I sort of had to fool around with
it on my own. For the most part I think they [the directions] were
well written; the only part that I didn't think was done well was the
illustration of this—I don't know what they call it, I guess it's a steam
adjustment valve. I couldn't tell which way to turn it as far as the
illustration went. They didn't show you to turn it this direction, turn
it that direction. That was a little confusing so I really had to test it
out on my own to see. [She refers to the diagrams in the instruction
booklet.] It depends on which way you're looking at the iron from.
And, it just doesn't make sense that this way will give you maximum
steam, and this way gives you medium steam, and as you get it here
it gives you continuous steam. [She is twisting the knob.] They
should give you continuous steam by the maximum side. That's just
the way it seems to me. Things like that confuse me. I just thought it
should have been a little bit more clearly illustrated. They should
have given you little photographs.

I thought the performance was very good. In the instruction booklet
it says that your steam power will be 10 times that of a regular
iron—and it is! It definitely, definitely is! Even if I have it at the
lowest setting there's still steam that comes out, it comes out
wonderfully, no problem, and you actually see the steam where in a
regular iron sometimes you don't see it. [With] this you see big
bursts of steam! So you'd better watch where your fingers are! I

really don't know why this one is so much less expensive [than the professional irons I've used]. I suppose these people [i.e., Simac] saw a need and they filled it by giving a less expensive professional iron. But the difference between them—I'm really not an expert. This [Simac] works the same in that the water is held in a separate tank. The professional iron isn't as cumbersome as this, it's just a flat surface with a little handle on it and a little knob for steam. But the professional irons that I've used don't have temperature settings; they set at one temperature and it's good for everything, while this [Simac] has the temperature settings for the different fabrics.

[She points to the reservoir and pad.] It wasn't hard to find a place to put this. I put it at the end of the ironing board, which you generally don't use anyway. But do you want to know a really nice feature that I saw? I'm left-handed, and the way my ironing board's set up, I go this way. [She goes through the motion of ironing as a left-hander.] And I can't put the iron here [on the pad] as you would normally, resting it like this [i.e., as a right-hander would do]. I have to rest it down like this. Being left-handed, it's sort of awkward. But this thing [the reservoir] comes up and adjusts out. [She swings the reservoir to another position for left-handed use.] Which is fabulous. They thought about me when they did it!

OK, about the cord, it's [explained] in the instruction booklet. The cord comes our really nice, like that. [She pulls both cords out.] So, do you remember I thought it was too short? But it's not, it's fine. Now if you're using it you leave it out. [She refers to the extended cords.] But I suppose if, I don't know, you're repositioning the iron, you just go inside here and turn here and it [the cords] closes right back up. [She lifts the pad and turns the cord rewind to recoil the cords snugly.] And it's really easy. You know, with normal irons you have to curl the ironing wire around the iron to put it away. I don't imagine this [coil rewind] will be any quicker but it makes it a lot neater. It winds really easy. I don't break my fingernails, which is nice.

And another nice feature is, with a regular conventional iron you put the water into the top of the iron and you can't really hold that much. This [reservoir] holds, I believe it said, a quart of water, which allows you enough steam to press three hours worth of ironing—not that I'm going to stand for three hours and iron anything, because I never would, but some people might. You just have to refill the water [once] in three hours worth of ironing.

Do you remember I was questioning about the small amount of steam vents? OK, they said [in the instruction booklet] it doesn't need any more steam vents to produce the ten times the amount of steam. It'll shoot the steam right in at a force 10 times greater than regular irons into the fabrics, so they [the fabrics] will get a little wet. So what happens is, from here down this [area with no vents] will act to dry the fabric a lot quicker than if you have an iron with all the steam vents because you'll have steam leaking from that [the additional vents on other models]. [She is pointing to the ironing surface of the Simac.] But this will make the fabric dry quicker, therefore speeding up the ironing! So I thought that was very interesting because [before] I thought, gee, how is that going to do the job that a regular iron does! I didn't see how it could do that.

But also in the booklet it said what you could do is you can have a garment hanging up and you just need to press the button and the steam just [does the job]. You don't have to have an ironing board and take your garment off and try to arrange it on the ironing board hoping you don't iron any new creases! Which is a really nice feature. It'll just steam the garment when it's hanging on the hanger. Say you get a wrinkle right here. [She points to her shoulder.] It's really difficult to press that. But, you just press the steam like this. See? Really easy.

In the back [of the instruction booklet] they give you ironing hints of the professionals which is nice since this is advertised as a professional iron. Hints and tricks. It's nice that they tell you some of these things. Most of it is common sense but it's nice that they would tell you. I read through it and found some of it kind of interesting.

It's hard to say if it's worth the price difference. It's faster [than my old iron] in that it does a better job with less strokes. I want to see how long it lasts. The iron that I have now I've had maybe eight years. I guess that's a good amount of time to get out of an iron. I don't know; I don't know; I don't know what the general life of an iron would be. But that [old] iron is very temperamental; it works when it wants to and it doesn't when it doesn't want to. And I'm hoping that I don't have that problem with this [new iron]. If this will continue to work, say for 10 or 15 years, work as good as on the first time I used it, then I'll say yes, it's worth it. I like the features that it has, so for that it's worth it. But again, I think it's a time test thing, like over how many years I'll see whether it was worth it or not. It *feels* good. It feels nice and weighty. This feels like it'll do the job.*

*Protocol was recorded by Stephen Bell.

CHOICE CRITERIA

Consumer choice may be based on nothing more than the intrinsic appeal of some product. In such a situation the consumer buys for no other reason beyond pleasing the senses and the emotions—liking the taste, sound, feel, smell, or perhaps seeking variety or satisfying curiosity. But most brand choices are not based purely on intrinsic preference. Although intrinsic appeal or intrinsic preference factors can constitute sufficient grounds for choice, other more objective reasons usually enter into consideration.

A consumer's want for a product is a want for something to produce certain effects or perform certain functions. (See Figure 8.) These functions can be categorized into the following five categories of choice criteria, which were also mentioned at the end of the last chapter:

1. *Technical functions* as reflected in choice criteria or reasons for buying concerned with product characteristics that contribute to performance like the speed, power, comfort, and reliability of a particular make of car.

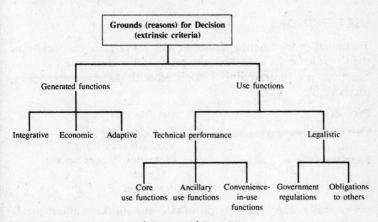

Figure 8 Use Functions and Generated Functions

2. *Legalistic functions* as reflected in choice criteria or reasons for buying concerned with product characteristics that contribute to meeting legal requirements (e.g., seatbelts) or the requests of other interested parties such as one's spouse.
3. *Integrative functions* as reflected in choice criteria concerned with the contribution the purchase makes to integrating consumers into their social milieu by taking account of fashion or convention or whatever helps the consumer integrate the purchase in with ego and status aspirations and/or social conscience.
4. *Economy functions* as reflected in choice criteria concerned with the functions of saving on costs—price, shopping time, and effort.
5. *Adaptive functions* as reflected in choice criteria concerned with the function of adapting to uncertainty about the costs and benefits associated with various buys.

In addition to the above categories of choice criteria, consumers consider the relative intrinsic appeal of brands. Intrinsic preference was discussed in Chapter 4. Hence, it will not be discussed here except to say that intrinsic preference factors may also enter the decision process when tradeoffs are required.

Not every choice is the result of a decision: decision presupposes deliberation. This bears repetition given the current vogue for using the word "decision" to cover every choice process.

USE FUNCTIONS

Technical (performance) factors focus on criteria that relate to the *use function(s)* for which the product was designed. Core use functions are those mainly associated with the class of product, for example

Product	Use function
Car	Transportation
Clock	Time Measurement
Sunglasses	Protection of eyes against the sun
Shoes	Protection of feet

Generally, use functions dominate our thinking about products and define their product class. In other words, items that share the same use function are grouped together in the same product class. Thus, anything counts as a coffee percolator if its use function is to percolate coffee and anything is a seat if its use function is to be sat on. When we speak of some product being "a good one," we are usually making reference to how well it fulfills its core use function. For example, the term "good watch" usually means "accurate timepiece."

Products that have several distinct use functions may give rise to ambiguity as to what constitutes a good one of its kind. Markets can be defined on the basis of the use function sought by those in the market. In such a case, the more clearly the manufacturer can establish the market use function, the more precisely can performance requirements be laid down. Performance requirements may not be obvious. Thus, what exactly is required of a paper towel? While rivals stressed absorbency, Viva won market share by stressing durability. Similarly, while rivals stressed how well their brands cleaned cars, Turtle Wax won market share in Sweden and Britain by stressing protection.

In considering use functions, the consumer's preferred technical criteria may be supplemented or even replaced by criteria emanating from outside bodies considered to have a legitimate right to influence the consumer's choice. We have termed these additional criteria "legalistic criteria." Generally, but not always, legalistic criteria are technical criteria associated with use functions.

GENERATED FUNCTIONS

Technical and legalistic criteria are concerned with use functions. Integrative, economic, and adaptive criteria are associated with *generated functions*. Generated functions are the costs and benefits associated with the products that are over and above the use function benefits. They arise through buying, using, consuming, or simply possessing the product. Thus, a living room chair is judged not simply on its use function as a sturdy, comfortable seat but also on how it will be perceived by others, whether it is fashionable (or too fashionable!), whether its price is too high (or too low), how rapidly it will reach obsolescence, and so on.

Generated functions reflect integrative, economic, and adaptive choice criteria. These, in turn, can be the key advantages of some products.

EXTRINSIC FACTORS IN BRAND SELECTION

Rival brands possess the same use function but are likely to perform that function with different degrees of efficiency. Even if rival brands perform use functions equally as well, they are likely to differ with respect to generated functions. For example, two different brands of shoes may equally protect the feet but be radically different in fashion and price.

Where brand choice involves deliberation on objective reasons for choice, these reasons are embodied in the use of technical, legalistic, integrative, economic, and adaptive criteria. The factors considered under these headings are termed *extrinsic preference* factors to distinguish their status from the mere subjective appeal considered under intrinsic preference (Von Wright, 1963). Although competition among brands is usually on the basis of extrinsic preference factors, however, as we have seen intrinsic preference may, on occasion, be decisive.

The varying emphasis given by different consumers to intrinsic factors, use functions, and generated functions gives rise to different market segments. A problem for the manufacturer is to find which wanted functions the firm can meet better than competition.

TECHNICAL CRITERIA

Technical (performance) criteria are concerned with factors that relate to product use. Even choices made on the basis of intrinsic preference (e.g., taste) may still consider technical criteria. For example, in buying a drink the consumer may take account of calories. We can distinguish three classes of use function:

1. *Core use function.* The core use function of toothpaste is to clean teeth and that of a laundry detergent to clean clothes. Core use functions in general are equated with the design function. However, although a product may be designed specifically to perform a certain function, it may not be used to perform that function. There may be a need to check whether the design function and the actual use to which a product is put are the same.

2. *Ancillary use functions.* Products are often associated with certain ancillary use functions. Such use functions may be an inevitable result of using the product or may be an added feature. For example, toothpaste may clean the mouth or the breath, whiten teeth, or reduce cavities by the addition of flour-

ide as a feature. Ancillary use functions constitute additional purposes served by the product.

3. *Convenience-in-use functions.* Consumers buy time by using brands that are more labor saving, easy or pleasant to use, or in some other way convenient. Recent examples are nail polish pens, shaving brushes with built-in lather, and toothpaste pumps (which consumers seem willing to buy at a 20% premium to avoid the "tyranny of the twist-off cap"). In the U.S., the sales of household products that require hard effort or are unpleasant to use (e.g., toilet bowl cleansers that require scrubbing) are well down while sales of alternatives (e.g., cleansers that scrub with each flush) are up. Cleaning liquids for cleaning bathrooms, and so on are replacing cleaning powders because they are more pleasant to use. Similarly, consumers want their detergent to be gentle on the hands and easy to measure and dispense.

Consumer Indifference to Added Performance

Technical performance criteria embrace all those physical attributes and performance characteristics that appear relevant to core use functions, ancillary use functions, and user problems. But not every consumer seeks the highest performance in each of these areas. There is a point in performance beyond which the consumer may be indifferent to added performance just as there is a point in watch accuracy and precision that serves no practical purpose for the consumer. For instance, a product that can only achieve better technical performance at the expense of aesthetic appeal (e.g., as with a water-repellent raincoat) may fail. Throughout the ages, fashionable clothes have been designed for both use functions and aesthetic and sex appeal.

Convenience-in-Use

It is possible for a product to have no core use function because, like a candy bar, it is bought purely on the basis of liking (intrinsic preference). But the product may still have a convenience-in-use function. For example, a novel may be bought for reading pleasure but the extent to which the layout, printing, and so on reduces reading effort may still be a factor in sales. Some books do have a core use-function to provide knowledge. But learning takes effort, and anything that reduces effort will contribute to sales. Easy-to-read books concerned with learning how to cope and how to manage one's life promise the reader painless solutions to deep problems. Such books provide rules for living better as well as emotional reassurance (i.e., the intrinsic appeal of reading about others in the same boat (Rychlak, 1979)). Where a book's topic is both unique and highly appealing, consumers seem prepared to tradeoff even the easy reading (convenience-in-use). For example, Oswald Spengler's prophetic book *Decline of the West* sold 100,000 copies when it first appeared in the 1920s in spite of an obscurity of prose that led one commentator to call it "A typical expression of the traditional German conviction that if a book is worth writing it is worth making it difficult to read."

Ancillary Use Function

Manufacturers may seek initially to compete on the basis of performance in core use functions. However, many a market leader has achieved its preeminence on the basis of performance in ancillary use functions (for example, Procter and Gamble's Crest toothpaste with flouride and Head & Shoulders shampoo with an anti-dandruff ingredient). As to minimizing user problems, we have the simplicity of the Brownie camera, the patented spout of Morton's salt, and the pop-up packaging of Kleenex tissues.

Product innovation is conceptually linked to the idea of performing use functions better or more fully. Improving use functions is probably the most basic strategy sought (though not necessarily achieved) to increase market share. Take the market for diapers: Procter & Gamble's Pampers once had 75% of the market, but Kleenex Huggies entered the market with a technically improved product to take a share of that market away. Procter & Gamble responded with Luvs, its own premium disposable diaper and with an improved version of Pampers. This war, fought on the basis of improved use functions, has reduced Procter & Gamble's market share to about 50%.

In some industries, there seems to be little hope that research will produce a technically superior product. A manufacturer who does bring out a technical improvement will create widespread interest. Thus, the personal care industry has had a poor record of product innovation which has stymied the growth of industry sales. However, the possibilities are there—witness the sales of Mousse, a styling foam for the hair, which achieved around $85 million in sales when first introduced in 1984.

Relationship Between Use Functions and Generated Functions

Although use functions and generated functions seem quite distinct conceptually, they are related. For example, technical criteria might serve to promote economic criteria. When Harley Procter put a groove in the middle of each soap bar, he added something to the technical characteristics of the product. But he had in mind the thrifty housewife who wanted to break the soap in half. Similarly, in an automobile fuel efficiency is a characteristic of the engine. As such, it is a technical characteristic even though it is instrumental to economic efficiency.

But economic and technical criteria are still distinct. Economic criteria refer to the consumer's costs or expenditures in money, shopping time, and shopping effort while technical criteria are concerned with what the consumer gets back in return. Some technical criteria serve to promote integrative criteria.

The demand for certain technical attributes may not be because such attributes are needed. In clothing, for example, people buy real leather flying jackets but never fly, buy ski clothing but never ski, and so on because possessing such things associates the wearer with prestigious pursuits. Similarly, consumers may want the latest technology in home computers even when it goes way beyond their anticipated uses—if it suggests being in the forefront of technology and being in a position to share names, jargon, and information. Finally, certain technical criteria might serve adaptive criteria in that buying the best technically might be perceived as a way of coping with uncertainty.

Surrogate Indicators of Likely Performance

Buyers do not always know the relative technical performance of brands. Thus, they are apt to fall back on surrogate indicators of likely performance, for example, "It also has a good, clean odor that gives me confidence that my dishes are clean." The consumer may believe that the presence of certain attributes is necessary for high performance. For example, the belief in Europe in the 1960s that boiling water was necessary to get clothes clean reduced the sales of automatic washers that used hot but not boiling water. It is essential in marketing a product to know how the consumer comes to infer the presence, absence, or level of performance of the desired attributes.

Certain product attributes may be regarded as a necessary condition for high performance. For example, the belief that wool is a necessary condition for quality in a suit rules out suits of man-made fibers for some people. One computer firm added sash weights to their home computer when they found its lightness suggested poor quality. Similarly, sales of lightweight vacuum cleaners were depressed because consumers believed heaviness was necessary for effectiveness.

The Relative Importance of the Functions

The relative importance attached to core use functions, ancillary use functions and convenience-in-use functions changes over time. For example, men's ties no longer serve the use function of protecting a man's shirt from food stains but perform the purely integrative functions of convention and fashion. Similarly, ancillary use functions may become less important. For example, housewives no longer worry the same about waxy, yellow build-up so that Johnson's Wax has sought to promote other functions as its critical advantage.

LEGALISTIC CRITERIA

The consumer's choice criteria can be constrained by the fear of sanctions arising from the violation of some code. Thus, consumer's might adhere to conventional norms in buying clothes because violating such norms leads to a diffuse set of *external* sanctions being applied by peer groups and others. Consumers may follow (as will be discussed in the next chapter) a code of integrity from fear of *internal* sanctions. Consumers may also adhere to the rules of some *specific* authority because that authority's rules are regarded as *legitimate* and violating them would lead to sanctions. Where adherence to such legitimate rules leads consumers to change or modify their normal criteria, we speak of their adhering to *legalistic criteria*.

In each of the above situations, fear of sanctions is the reason given for adhering to buying rules, but such fear is not the only reason. There are usually positive benefits arising from following convention, one's own moral code, or the demands of some legitimate authority. In the case of convention, consumers conform to be accepted by various social groups. In the case of personal integrity, there is the satisfaction of being true to oneself. In the case of adherence to the rules of some legitimate authority, there is the satisfaction of meeting obligations and promises. Here is how it breaks down:

Source of Constraint	Nature of Sanction	Nature of Incentive	
Convention	External, *diffuse* social sanctions	Integration/acceptance by society	Part of integrative criteria
Personal integrity	Internal (conscience)	Coherence with values and self-image	
Legitimate authority	External sanctions applied by a *specific* authority perceived as making legitimate demands	Satisfaction in meeting external obligations	Legalistic criteria

The most obvious forms of legitimate authority affecting the consumer's choice criteria are the various government bodies in a position to pass laws. The law may restrict choice by prohibiting the sale of certain products (e.g., drugs) that the consumer would otherwise buy. Or the law may restrict choice by limiting accessibility to certain products (e.g., handguns) to those authorized to buy them. The law may also affect choice by defining how a job is to be done (e.g., how a house is to be wired). The law may even dictate purchases that otherwise may not be made, such as snow tires, seat belts, and smoke alarms. In redirecting demand, legislation affects company fortunes. Thus, when legislation restricted phosphates in detergents, Procter & Gamble's technological lead was greatly eroded, as evidenced by the dramatic drop in its sales.

The government is not the only authority whose rules may be regarded as legitimate. A consumer may be buying for others or may feel obligated to take account of the legitimate interests of others so as not to disappoint them. When letting others down is painful, it acts as a sanction. Thus, an office may be decorated in neutral colors that do not offend anyone and the person doing the family shopping will try to consider each family member's favorite foods.

Consumers may even respond to what they believe are the interests of others even when it entails a lower level of personal welfare. This is particularly so when there is a belief that it means much more to the other person making the request. A husband may choose a house in the city, although he wants to live in the country, because where they live means more to his wife. Where a purchase decision is a joint decision, legalistic criteria enter into the deliberations of both parties when each takes account of the interests of the other. It is not a question of who has the power to enforce their will, but whether they would want to do so if it meant going against the strong preference of the other party.

Sometimes consumers buy according to what they believe others would want on the basis of what they themselves prefer. This frequently arises in buying for family members. Such self-reference can lead to error. Hence the advertisement showing the housewife suddenly coming to realize that what she had been buying all these years for her husband was not the brand he preferred.

SUMMARY

Although products can be bought purely on the basis of their intrinsic appeal, most products are also bought to perform functions. Objective reasons for choice describe the functions that are sought. Where consumer choice is based purely on objective reasons, choice is based on extrinsic preference. Apart from intrinsic appeal, a product is bought for its anticipated performance in one or more of the following five functions:

1. Technical use functions

2. Legalistic functions

3. Integrative functions

4. Adaptive functions

5. Economy functions

This chapter dealt with technical and legalistic functions.

Technical use functions relate to the use functions for which the product was designed.:

- Core use functions are the technical functions that tend to distinguish the product class (e.g., the core use function of clocks is to measure time).
- Ancillary use functions are the permanent or optional technical functions associated with the performance of the core use function (e.g., one ancillary use function of a detergent might be to soften clothes).
- Convenience-in-use functions are the additions, modifications, or packaging of a product that facilitate the performance of its core or ancillary use functions (e.g., furniture polish in an aerosol can, press-button telephones, battery-operated wall clocks, and so on).

Legalistic functions are those functions that are adopted by the consumer as choice criteria to meet what are regarded as the legitimate demands of others. Thus, the law may insist on certain functions being added to a product or consumers may follow the choice criteria of others whose interests they feel obligated to consider.

IMPLICATIONS FOR MARKETING

1. If the marketing strategy is to take account of consumer motivations, the firm needs to identify the choice criteria the consumer employs or might be persuaded to employ together with information on how the consumer judges the presence of the choice criteria.

2. The firm should seek to identify choice criteria by collecting protocol statements that record the thoughts of consumers
   (a) Before the buy
   (b) During the buy
   (c) After the buy
   by interpreting the key words or concepts used by consumers as reflecting the rules or choice criteria they use to guide their choice of brand.

3. The firm should classify the choice criteria into six categories that reflect the functions for which the product is being sought, namely
   (a) Intrinsic functions
   (b) Technical functions
   (c) Legalistic functions
   (d) Integrative functions
   (e) Economy functions
   (f) Adaptive functions
   This chapter deals with the first three functions.

4. The firm should subdivide technical functions into
   (a) Core use functions
   (b) Ancillary use functions
   (c) Convenience-in-use functions

5. The firm should
   (a) Creatively devise new ways of enhancing core use functions or add additional ancillary and convenience-in-use benefits as these may fill some gap in the market and provide a critical advantage.
   (b) Ensure that the use function for which the product was designed coincides with the use function for which it is being used.
   (c) Establish the required performance that is sought in the core

use function since adding to performance may add nothing to demand. Any additional performance may be incompatible with achieving adequate performance on the other functions while adding a great deal to the cost.

(d) Discover how consumers actually infer performance levels so the firm can use this information as a basis for product modification and promotional appeals.

(e) Recognize that the relative importance attached to core use functions, ancillary use functions and convenience-in-use functions varies over time so that product and sales appeals are updated.

(f) Recognize that brands that appear to be bought purely on the basis of liking (intrinsic preference) may have their value enhanced by the addition of convenience-in-use.

6. The firm should identify the legalistic criteria that is followed by consumers to meet what are regarded as the legitimate demands of others, namely,

(a) Governmental legislation

(b) Spouses, parents, and others whose interests are affected by the buying decision

Such criteria may be unaffected by persuasive communications.

Comment on Protocol Statement for Purchase of Vapor Simac Steam Iron

1. GOAL(S)

i. *Vision:* To be beautiful not ugly.
ii. *Social:* To signal to others her preferred self-image and to save time through the use of a fast steam iron.

2. WANT(S)

The consumer wanted a replacement iron but in particular wanted a professional steam iron.

i. The brochure she received for the $250 professional steam iron activated a latent want for such an iron but it remained passive awaiting her saving for it.
ii. The advertisement for the less expensive Vapor Simac on sale at $100 activated the passive want for some sort of a professional iron.

3. BELIEFS

i. A professional iron would further her goals more than a conventional iron.
ii. She knew enough about a professional iron to know about its superior performance.
iii. She did not believe in paying more than $150 for the Vapor Simac when she could get a fully professional model for $250.
iv. A professional iron for the extra price would:
    (a) Be more reliable in terms of steam generation.
    (b) Use distilled water which reduces the risk of mineral water spots on clothes with the water being distilled by the Vapor Simac from tap water.

      (c) Save time with much less work.

      (d) Press clothes more easily.

      (e) Get wrinkles out better.

  v. The difference between the Vapor Simac at $100 and a fully professional iron at $250 is probably too small to be worth paying the difference for performance.

  vi. The sale of the Vapor Simac by Macy's influenced the timing of the purchase by her belief that it was a bargain.

  vii. Macy's is an acceptable outlet for buying steam irons.

4. CHOICE CRITERIA

Technical Functions

  i. Core use function: To iron out wrinkles giving a professional look. The consumer was unable to directly evaluate either the level of performance or the reliability of performance on this core use function. She inferred the effectiveness of the Vapor Simac in the core use function from:

      (a) Surface similarity of the Vapor Simac to the fully professional iron

      (b) Numer of steam vents (although this indicator proved ambiguous)

      (c) Temperature settings for various types of fabrics

      (d) Contrast with the conventional Sunbeam iron with its plastic parts and lightness

  ii. Ancillary use functions:

      Vapor Simac could be used on hanging garments

  iii. Convenience-in-use functions:

      (a) Ease of using knobs

      (b) Convenience in being able to use tap water

      (c) Convenience of pad for resting iron

      (d) Safety

Integrative Functions

Convention and fashion played no role in the buying decision. However, there are hints that the buyer might derive some sense of status from being the first among her acquaintances to own such an iron.

Economy Functions

The buyer did trade off what she perceived to be the greater technical performance of the fully professional iron for the lower cost of the

Vapor Simac. She also held certain expectations as to the extra value that should be provided by the $100 iron over the conventional iron sold at a much lower price. Her reserve price for the Vapor Simac was $150 and for a super professional model she was disposed to pay up to $250. As far as irons were concerned, she believed that price and quality were positively related.

Adaptive Functions

Adaptive criteria were very important to this buyer because even though the iron performed an important function for her, the product was expensive. She recognized that she did not know a lot about irons. However, any anxiety she had about buying was somewhat relieved by

  i. Macy's policy of accepting returns.
 ii. The toll-free telephone number on the package to call in the event of a complaint.
iii. The opportunity to handle the product.
 iv. Her identification of the Vapor Simac with the professional irons she had used in the past—inferred from the subtitle on the box ("professional ironing system").

Strangely, she did not give much weight to brand name or country of origin as symbols of reassurance. It may be that she assumed it was enough of a guarantee that Macy's stocked the brand.

Intrinsic Appeal

The consumer was not "crazy about" the product's "looks." But she weighted this of little importance because the product was not a socially visible one.

Decision-Making

In terms of her decision-making, the buyer could be inconsistent and given to wishful thinking. For instance, she initially argued that the true professional iron was lighter than the conventional iron, but later claimed that weight was an indicator of quality. Similarly, although she seemed to believe that the more vents in the iron the better, her wishful thinking in respect to the Vapor Simac led her to entertain the very opposite belief. In the decision process, her priorities on technical criteria seemed to shift from reliability, to effectiveness, to durability. In her retrospective account, she inferred the product's effectiveness in part by equating more visible steam with more powerful steam.

The buyer was sensitive to the fact that no evaulation (such as an in-store examination) was adequate without actually using the product. Macy's liberal returns policy allowed her to try the product at home before actually resolving to keep it.

Implications for Marketing

If this consumer was representative of prospective buyers of Vapor Simac, there are certain implications for marketing. In general, technical and adaptive criteria are the consumer's dominant choice criteria, and the firm's marketing strategy should recognize this fact.

1. Product
   i. Core use function: If this consumer is representative, consumers infer steam power from steam visibility. It may be possible to enhance such visibility by repositioning or redirecting the steam vents. However, efforts along these lines must be balanced with genuine performance considerations.

   The weight of the iron might be modified to fall in line with the weight that most signals quality. Styling needs to be investigated to fit the product image of being professional and "high tech." Even though the buyer was prepared in this instance to dismiss the importance of appearance, this does not mean that appropriate styling would not have contributed value for the consumer.
   ii. Ancillary use functions: Any ancillary use functions that extend the range and scope of the core use function are likely to be an advantage.
   iii. Convenience-in-use functions: The firm should investigate the buyer's complaints about the continuous steam setting being illogically located and the booklet having confusing instructions.

   A lighter iron makes for user convenience. Ideally, lightness should be sought as part of the design and sold as an advantage. However, lightness (as stated earlier) might encounter a perception problem by suggesting lower quality.
2. Promotion
   i. The aim of any promotional campaign would be both to attract new users of steam irons and convert customers when replacing their old conventional iron.
   ii. The want for the professional iron among consumers is likely to be latent. Hence, there will be a need to educate them about the technical performance advantages of a professional iron and the Vapor Simac iron in particular:
   (a) Saving in time
   (b) Ease of use

      (c) Use on hard-to-iron fabrics
      (d) Versatility
      (e) Professional image
      (f) Equally suitable for left- and right-handed people
      (g) Fewer vents for speed of drying

  iii. There will be a need to anticipate and overcome perceptions about
      (a) Product complexity
      (b) High price

  iv. Any well-publicized innovation in a mature market not subject to heavy brand advertising is likely to attract considerable consumer attention. It is possible that the product could obtain a good deal of free publicity prior to the major advertising campaign.

  v. The packaging and the instruction booklet should describe and explain the iron's functions and features and address potential customer reservations (e.g., about the cord, steam vents, place on the ironing board for the pad and water reservoir, and so on). The consumer needs to know exactly what constitutes the total system being offered for sale.

  vi. Although the above will help the consumer cope with uncertainties about the product, the firm might
      (a) Use point-of-sale demonstrators
      (b) Quote the relevant statistics showing Vapor Simac superiority
      (c) Provide opportunities to try the product prior to final commitment

3. Price
Although the buyer was willing to pay more than the sale price and while a premium price is consistent with consumer expectations about a product that promises so much, there is nonetheless a need to demonstrate that the cost to the consumer is an investment with a high payoff.

4. Distribution and Service
  i. A push selling strategy is likely to be needed as consumers will probably be skeptical about the manufacturer's claims.

  ii. An exclusive distribution system consisting of high class retail outlets is required.

  iii. Retail outlets should
      (a) Have trained sales personnel to anticipate and deal with doubts and objections
      (b) Provide service including a liberal returns policy

7

Grounds for Deciding: Integrative, Adaptive, and Economic Criteria

The final three categories of choice criteria—integrative, adaptive, and economic—are discussed here. As in Chapter 6, however, the reader is first presented with a protocol statement. This time, it is a protocol given by a businessman purchasing a computer for his small business. The reader should analyze the protocol before going on to read the discussion of the criteria. Readers should try to identify the goals, wants, beliefs, and choice criteria and the implications for marketing management, assuming this buyer's behavior is typical of those in the market segment. Again, readers might wish to rethink their analyses after reading this chapter as a way of assessing its utility. An analysis of the protocol is given in Appendix B to this chapter so that readers can check whether the concepts discussed are sufficiently operational to make for reliable interpretation.

Protocol Statement on the Buying of an IBM Personal Computer

Introduction

The following is a protocol statement by the owner of a small business describing how he came to buy an IBM personal computer. It is of interest because of the special role played by integrative and adaptive criteria. There are usually major differences between consumer buying and buying for an organization such as a business firm.

In the first place, the buying organization is usually selecting a supplier and not just making a one-time purchase. This means that the categories of buying criteria (technical, economic, legalistic, integrative, and adaptive) have to be reinterpreted somewhat to apply to organizational buying.

In the second place, several people may be involved in the decision-making process. Each of these participants may exercise different degrees of influence and weight the various sets of buying criteria differently, so there is a problem of predicting what choice criteria and ranking will emerge to dominate the decision.

Finally, although the individual participants have individual and professional goals that can influence their choice criteria, there are nonetheless certain superordinate, organizational goals against which to evaluate the offerings of rival suppliers. These superordinate goals, which are listed below, are concerned with seizing opportunities or solving problems:

Seizing Opportunities To

- Increase the efficiency of operations.
- Enhance sales or saleability.
- Protect the organization's assets.
- Increase the firm's flexibility.

Solving Problems Involving

- Material/component shortages.
- Obsolescent/old equipment.
- New project needs.
- Poorly performing current suppliers.

In the following protocol statement the complications of group decision-making do not occur. The proprietor alone makes the buying decision. Because the actual process of buying a computer occurred over an extended period of time, the contemporaneous account was based on immediate recall after each stage. However, the example is included because of the richness of the buyer's recall, the topical interest of the purchase, and the fact that the buyer was asked to note his thoughts at each stage in the buying process.

Anticipatory Account

I own a small clothing store and employ eight people. Currently, all of the store's recordkeeping is done manually. My business is growing and the recordkeeping is becoming a problem. I am also thinking of buying another store in the next year or so.

I'm pretty sure a computer could help me with my current operation. Some of my business associates and friends have bought computers and claim they have been a big help. My associates specifically mentioned the areas of Accounts Receivable, Accounts Payable and General Ledger.

Every time I pick up a magazine or newspaper there is an article about computers. I see television commercials about computers from many companies. But I feel a void because I don't know the details as to how a computer works or how it could help me. I feel like everyone is jumping on the computer bandwagon and I am being left behind.

I never have been a technical person and I have a fear that I will not be able to use the computer properly. I can't even type. I'm not sure how much a computer for my business would cost. My friends told me that it would cost between $5,500 and $7,000. But I have heard stories of people spending $6,000 for the computer and then spending $20,000 to have someone program it and it still didn't work. This possibility really scares me. But despite my concerns I felt I had to make an attempt to understand what a computer could do to help me run my business.

Contemporaneous Account

I had seen a commercial about "Computerland Stores" where people walk right off the street to see computers. So I decided to visit one and talk to a salesman. A salesman came over and introduced himself. I explained to him my situation, my general areas of concern, and gave him a quick overview of my operation. I made it clear that I knew nothing about computers. He took down some notes while I was speaking. He then suggested that I pick up the latest issue of *Personal Computing,* browse through it and set up an appointment to meet again next week. In the meantime, he would do some groundwork on what computer might be best for me and the approximate costs. He would also demonstrate the computer for me.

The salesman seemed competent so I decided to keep the next appointment. I appreciated the fact that he didn't try to force a computer down my throat. Instead he took time to analyze what computer would be best for me.

I browsed through *Personal Computing* but it didn't help. In fact I became more confused by the large number of ads for hundreds of different products. I hoped that the salesman could narrow down the choices for me.

I became more attentive watching TV when computer commercials came on. I saw the IBM commercial with "Charlie Chaplin." I liked it and thought it was well done. Also the commercial depicted someone who needed help with his business and got it with the IBM Personal Computer.

At the second meeting we [the salesman and I] talked in more detail about my business operation and my current and future plans. I mentioned what my associates had said about the areas of AR, AP, and General Ledger. I told him that I didn't understand how a computer could help me run my operation.

The salesman explained that the computer could certainly handle AR, AP, and General Ledger, and in doing so provide me with more up-to-date information. He spoke about the savings that could result from keeping a tighter control of AR and AP.

He then spoke about the additional advantages that a computer can offer. He said that by keeping a tighter control of inventory I could avoid stock outs. This would result in fewer lost sales and allow for a smoother business operation. The computer could also produce mailings to regular customers to let them know about sales. This idea appealed to me because I always like it when the "big" department stores like Barney's send me a similar mailing. The computer could produce cash and sales projections that currently I do by hand, in a much shorter time. He added that the computer could handle a lot of my typing requirements. While I wouldn't buy a computer because it can type, I'm glad to know that it does have that capability. He said also that if I did buy that second store I might not have to hire another bookkeeper because all of the recordkeeping could be controlled from the main store.

At this point I was very impressed with the salesman. He had done his homework and had raised my awareness level of what a computer can do for me.

Up to now it all sounded wonderful. But I still had two big concerns: How much will this cost, and could I operate the computer effectively?

The salesman gave me three possible computer choices that would meet my needs: IBM, Apple, and Televideo. I told him to forget about Televideo because I had never heard of the company. But I have heard of Apple and certainly of IBM. He then quoted the price including software: the Apple would run about $6,100; the IBM would be about $6,700. The salesman said he preferred the IBM and said it was the best selling personal computer. He said he owned one himself and was worth the extra money. He mentioned how the computer can be fully depreciated for tax purposes and in addition Investment Tax Credit can be taken. This was certainly good news.

He proceeded at this point to show me the two computers: The IBM Personal Computer (PC) and the Apple IIe. I preferred the look and feel of the PC. It was sturdier and had a sleek design. The PC felt and looked solid. The Apple looked and felt "plasticy." It looked cheap. I preferred the IBM PC keyboard, which is maneuverable. The Apple's keyboard is physically attached to the rest of the system. Also the PC keyboard made a light clicking sound when I hit the keys. The Apple keys made no sound so I wasn't sure if I had hit the key hard enough.

At this point, I was leaning toward the PC. It was clear that the salesman, who I felt was knowledgeable, preferred the PC. My associates spoke highly of the PC; plus the fact that IBM has such a great reputation as a company. I knew that IBM would be around for a long time. I wasn't that sure about Apple. I have always been happy with my IBM typewriters. And whenever they needed repair the service was excellent. In addition, the possible tax break made the difference in price between the PC and the Apple unimportant. I had decided at this point that if I did buy a computer it would be the IBM PC. I told this to the salesman but added that my only concern left was whether I could effectively use the PC. He assured me this would not be a problem.

He sat down with me in front of the PC to begin what he called a "hands-on" demonstration. He explained the various components and let me turn the PC on. He showed me how to load a software package called PFS: FILE that could keep a file of all my customers, of my inventory and generate mailing lists. He showed me how to create a file of customers and to enter their names. We then printed out a mailing to each of the customers with their name on it. I thought that this was great. But what I was most excited about was that I was actually using a computer and enjoying it. I began to feel that I could operate this damn machine. The hands-on technique was an excellent method of helping me to overcome my fear of computers.

He then showed me the manual for the General Ledger software package and told me how easy it is to learn and use it. The manual was written in plain English with easy-to-follow diagrams and examples.

I would have liked to continue, but I had to return to my store. We arranged for another meeting on Friday. I left the store feeling very good about the idea of buying a PC.

On Friday I returned to the store and the salesman sat me down at the PC and showed me another software package he thought would be helpful. It was called LOTUS 1 2 3, which he described as the best of the "electronic spreadsheet" packages. He showed me how to do future cash flow projections with LOTUS. What impressed me the most was what he termed the "what if" capability of LOTUS. We did a cash flow analysis with several columns of numbers and assumed a 10% inflation rate. Then we changed it to a 5% inflation rate by changing just one number and every column of numbers was automatically recalculated to reflect the new inflation rate. He asked me how long would it have taken me to do the recalculation and I told him at least an hour.

The salesman pointed out that software packages like PFS: FILE and LOTUS 1 2 3 are written by independent software companies and that more programs like these are being written specifically for the IBM PC than for any other small computer.

The salesman told me that IBM provides a 90-day warranty and a service contract can be signed through the Computerland Store. He then offered me two free classes taught at the store on how to use LOTUS and the General Ledger packages in common business applications.

At this point, there was nothing left but to sign the sales order. I had finally decided to enter the computer age. The salesman told me he could have [the computer] delivered to my store in two weeks.

Retrospective Account

The PC was easy to set up. The directions were clear and there really wasn't that much to do. The setting up of some of my initial files took longer than I thought, but I considered it a learning experience. My workers at first were scared to operate it but I made sure they sat down and used it until they felt more comfortable with the PC.

Although I have only had the PC for three weeks I would say that I am very happy with my decision to buy the PC. I feel confident that it will help me better run my store.*

*Protocol was recorded by Anthony Lofrumento.

GENERATED FUNCTIONS

In evaluating alternative products or brands, the consumer does so in terms of the differential effects (i.e., costs and benefits) associated with each option. In the last chapter, we dealt with use function benefits (i.e., technical and legalistic criteria). Here we discuss the costs and benefits that are over and above the performance of use functions. (See Figure 9.) In taking account of such generated functions, the consumer makes use of three additional choice criteria:

1. *Integrative criteria.* In using integrative criteria to evaluate options, people judge the extent to which the different options contribute toward integrating them into the social system and enhance their sense of personal worth.
2. *Economic criteria.* Economic criteria take account of the sacrifices (money, time, and effort) attached to each option.
3. *Adaptive criteria.* In applying adaptive criteria, the consumer comes to terms with (adapts to) the various uncertainties attached to the options to reduce the risk emanating from a lack of information.

INTEGRATIVE CRITERIA

Where integrative (choice) criteria enter into a decision, the consumer evaluates a product by the extent to which it strengthens a sense of social belonging and standing with others and is consistent with the consumer's desired self-image and sense of per-

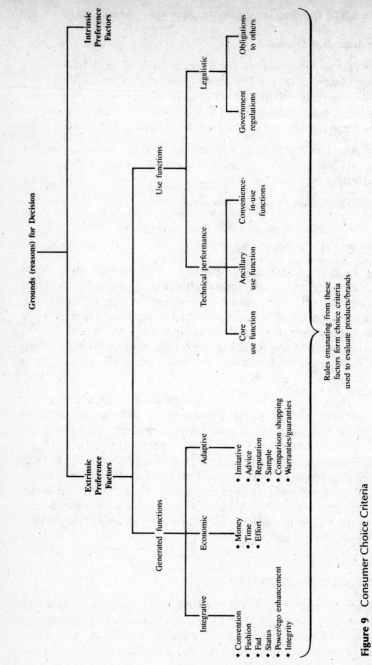

Figure 9 Consumer Choice Criteria

sonal integrity. Consumers may also enhance their belonging and standing with others by applying legalistic criteria, but that is not their primary reason. The primary reason is to satisfy obligations stemming from the legitimate demands of others. Integrative criteria are dominant in dress, home furnishings, and decoration. Clothes, jewelry, handbags, hairstyles, cosmetics, carpets, bedroom, dining room, and kitchen furniture are not bought just for their utility in terms of comfort, durability, and other use functions but also as a signal to the world of the consumer's status, values, self-image, and so on.

Advertising plays a major role in signalling how the advertised brand facilitates the buyer's integration into the community or with self. Advertisers refer to advertising's "added values" to mean advertising's capacity to increase the desire for and satisfaction with a product by magnifying the consumer's actual or anticipated subjective experiences of socially belonging, having status, and so on (Marchand, 1985). It might also be claimed that associating the product with animated characters like Mr. Clean, Speedy Alka Seltzer, or the Green Giant feeds the fantasy of having a personal relationship with the product.

Social Integration

In a market situation where all competitors emphasize technical criteria, a firm can often find a lucrative niche by focusing on integrative criteria. For example, in the market for sunglasses, competitors like Cool Ray chose quality optics and other technical criteria to be the core of their sales appeal, while Foster-Grant successfully emphasized the glamour of their glasses.

When a product has high social visibility (like sunglasses) consumers are apt to seek social validation of whatever they buy. But approval by peer groups is a minimal requirement since people also seek to generate admiration, respect, and even envy through their purchases—while at the same time satisfying a private self. Sometimes additional social integration is rejected as being in conflict with the private self since succumbing completely to the pressures of social life is a sacrifice of individuality. For example, social integration can demand expensive entertaining that may be inconsistent with the consumer's ideas about social living.

Consumers seek social integration by considering convention, fashion, fads, and status and power when making purchases. Consumers seek integration with self in their purchases by thinking about their personality needs. In sum, integrative criteria arise whenever consumers consider

Social expectations
Their desire for status, rank, and power
The demands of their conscience

Integrative criteria are often regarded as emotionally based. But convention, fashion, and status considerations can be part of a rational buying plan and not just a reactive impulse action as suggested by the word "emotional." Products signal to others the owner's rank, values, and preferred self-image—and consumers are prepared to pay a heavy price for ensuring social acceptance. There is "emotional buying," of course, as evaluations in buying can stimulate deep feelings about the uncertainties and anticipated benefits, but buying that is based mainly on integrative criteria does not necessarily fall into that category.

Convention

Convention is not something that just arises from historical agreement. It is a regularity or rule which offers benefits to each member of the group to which it applies. The convention of driving on only one side of the road (left or right) is one example. Conventions arise when a group has a problem of coordination that is best solved by each member of the group adhering to some regularity. Consumers trade the pleasure of making a completely independent choice for the social acceptance arising from having their actions coordinated with others within their social milieu. A regularity is conventional if people conform to it and expect others to conform to it for the sake of coordination (Lewis, 1969).

Both product and brand choices are influenced by social conventions. In adhering to these conventions, consumers meet the expectations of others. Their behavior becomes more predictable. This, in turn, makes it easier for people to interact and coordinate their actions. If people are to be accepted and liked, they are expected to fall into line and not act up. A deviant from convention, for example someone who dressed like Liberace for a funeral or in workmen's overalls to be a bridegroom, would not be coordinating his or her actions with others, thus giving rise to inappropriate action or embarrassment on the part of others.

Choices based on convention can be distinguished from choices based on habit. Buying in accordance with convention, unlike habit, does not stem from any initial deliberation but evolves from the process of socialization. However, although convention may sometimes lead to automatic choice because sticking to the rules of one's social milieu may be considered of paramount importance, knowledge of the conventional thing to do is usually just one input into the buying decision.

Some conventions, like shaking hands on being introduced, are part of the general culture, but others belong to a particular subculture, social class, age, occupation, or region of the country. Hence, deliberately not conforming to the conventions of society-at-large may still be conformative behavior to the norms of some group. However, there are social generalizations. For example, older people tend not to be fashion innovators nor opinion leaders in fashion. Generally, they are the last to adopt and the last to give up a mode of dress. Convention dictates that people "dress their age" and social sanctions are applied to those who do not.

Conventions are socially enforced as failure to conform (e.g., to standards of cleanliness) evokes unfavorable reactions from others. (See studies on group influence in buying, Bourne, 1957; Venkatesan, 1966; and Moschis, 1976.) People seek to become familiar with the appropriate conventions, as evidenced by books on wedding etiquette and good manners as well as by letters to advice columnists. Advertising recognizes this anxiety to do the right thing. By claiming something to be typical there is the hope it will be regarded as conventional, for example

> The American breakfast, no mistake, starts with sugar, milk, and Kellogg's cornflakes.

More commonly, advertising may appeal to social shame or fear of social ostracism, for example, by suggesting social conventions are being violated by not using a mouthwash, not feeding children the right food, or not celebrating some event. As far as social matters are concerned, many consumers seem only too relieved to follow the advice of experts on what is socially correct. People, it seems, will happily write for advice to fictitious personal advisers set up by firms to promote their products.

Conventions change as they come into conflict with either new beliefs about the need for flexibility or new ways of expressing goals and wants. Consider the following situations:

The dress conventions imposed on women in the past conflicted with the current belief that women should have more freedom to choose their clothes.

The conventions associated with weddings have been altered by fewer people choosing a church ceremony and the increasing number of second and third marriages.

However, conventions about the type of house chosen, its location, the furniture in it, what one eats, how one eats, what occasions are celebrated, what clothes are worn, what hairstyle is adopted, and so on are still very much constrained by the conventions of one's social milieu.

Fashion

Consumer choice can be influenced by fashion. In affluent Western societies, fashion and convenience-in-use have been the two attributes of most interest to the consumer since the end of World War II. Adopting the latest fashion in dress signals social aspiration, and attracts admiration and esteem. Consumers want to keep up with the Joneses; they want to avoid being considered behind the times or old sticks-in-the-mud. The very latest in high fashion clothes is expensive, however, and not everyone feels pressure to have them. However, there are fashions other than haute couture that occur at other levels and within other social groups, so that few people—even children in elementary school—escape its influence entirely.

When high fashion filters down as cheaper copies spread, the style becomes less fashionable among those who first adopted it. Part of the satisfaction from fashion is the pleasure from sharing scarce information about the changing social scene, but a major satisfaction is the fantasy. As one fashion expert worded it, "Fashion allows us to become temporarily what we are not—to slip into new identities. It enables us to camouflage our deficiencies and exaggerate our attributes. It is an outlet for our creative impulses."

Lurie (1983) in a popular book on fashion argues that people, through fashion, seek to tie themselves to sources of power and influence:

1. *Glamour figures.* Many teenagers wore a sequinned glove or a multi-zippered jacket to emulate pop star Michael Jackson's dress. Now we find the same phenomena with Madonna as teenagers wear crucifixes, lace boots, lacey bows in their hair, and skinny tops with bare midriff. At the peer group level, such a gesture makes for a sense of camaraderie as it is a declaration of values and identifications. At the individual level, the gesture evokes the fantasy of being glamorous.
2. *Adventurous activities.* Occupations and sports that require high skills, scarce personal qualities, and involve suspense and danger (e.g., space travel, flying, hand-to-hand combat, macho sports, and so on), generate fashion as people adopt the symbols of what they admire. If anyone should doubt people's capacity to fantasize about relationships through some remote association, we need only note the identification of football fans with their local teams—even when the team does not include a hometown player.
3. *Lifestyles reflecting nostalgia, glamour, or prestige.* Those countries that are admired for their power and material success are copied by less affluent nations. The fashions of American youth, for example, are popular in all continents. U.S. jeans, for example, are often a prized fashion symbol as if owning the symbol is being part of the U.S.A. Nostalgia, too, plays a role. Young adults often adopt childhood fashions (many vacation clothes are adult versions of children's clothes). City dwellers who dress in country clothes on weekends may also be expressing a nostalgic identification.
4. *National mood.* National mood, reflecting how well the economy is doing, how threatened the country is, and the confidence with which people can look to the future, seems to influence fashion. Examples include:

National Mood	Reflection in Fashion
Anxious	Serious, conservative dress, plain classics, shorter hairstyles (as signs of conformity and self-restraint).

National Mood	Reflection in Fashion
Rebellious	Outrageous dress (the punk rock look).
Nostalgic	Backward looking, like the expensive boarding school "preppy" look with its heavy fabrics and old-fashioned designs.

Fashion in dress may conflict with use function since being fashionable frequently means sacrificing comfort and durability. If blue jeans were once comfortable working trousers, today's expensive, skin-tight designer jeans ensure that comfort is again sacrificed for glamour.

Lurie views dress as being analogous to speech, for example,

- Casual dress, like casual speech, tends to be colorful.
- Interjecting the odd foreign garment, like using the odd foreign word, suggests social sophistication.
- Just as the meaning of a word changes with the context, so does the meaning of an item of dress change with the occasion on which it is being worn.
- Just as significant occasions demand more stylized speech so do significant social roles require people to dress for them.
- Just as there can be lying in speech there can be deception in dress.
- Just as every communication carries not only a message but also a tone, the pattern and color of dress correspond to tone of voice. Thus, certain tones and certain colors are suited to some occasions and not to others.

Colors, too, have certain connotations in every society. In western society, colors have the following meanings:

White: delicacy
Black: mourning/business
Red: strength and vitality
Yellow: youth, hope, and cheer
Blue: harmony, honesty, calmness
Green: outdoors, country life
Brown: friendliness, trust, reliability

But reaction to color is tied to culture and fashion. In primitive societies, as Humphrey (1983) points out, colors seem to be universally ranked for preference in blue, green, yellow, red order. While all colors are used to catch attention, transmit information, affect emotions, and so on, the color red is the most ambiguous since it can be both inviting (e.g., red lips) or threatening (e.g., sight of blood). Perhaps this is why red was so extensively used by armies in past centuries. A good deal of literature on the psychology of color has evolved since the 1920s when studies were made investigating color preferences by sex, class, and feelings aroused (Poffenburger 1925).

There was an initial reluctance to introduce color into such utilitarian products as bath towels and phones, as if color introduced a discordant note into a serious activity. Henry Ford's famous remark telling customers they could have any color providing it was black was only equalled by his objection to the indtroduction of stylistic fashion "into the serious business of transportation." He once declared "We are no longer in the automobile but in the millinery business." Yet the introduction of style and color has been one way of increasing the individual demand for products such as men's shirts, women's purses, shoes, and stockings.

Status Pressures

Kron (1983) neatly captures the social pressures on those in the U.S. who seek "the upward status passage." They quickly learn, for example, that in upper class circles people do not serve jello molds, buy plastic flowers, or use antimacassars on sofas. They learn to choose Crabtree and Evelyn soaps rather than Ivory soap, and so on.

Those aspiring to the upper class feel the need to turn to experts for advice. Top designers act as "gatekeepers" in certifying what constitutes good taste. Naturally, good taste costs a lot of money! Frequent changes are mandated to ensure expert help is constantly in demand, for example high pile carpets out, flat pile carpets in; flowered bed linens out, antique, lace-trimmed linens in; and so on.

The most damning judgment is to be considered dated as this implies not being ahead of what is happening on the social scene. All this may be true of some people aspiring to climb the social ladder. However, there are, no doubt, others belonging to the old monied upper class who would despise all this and reject the latest fashions as reflecting nouvelle riche insecurity.

The Fashionable Image

The cosmetics industry has a foot in fashion since it, too, caters to cyclical views about how deficiencies can be camouflaged and new identities assumed. But the fashionable image more directly symbolizes an enviable lifestyle and a dream self-image. Nonetheless not every seemingly enviable image becomes fashionable. The trick is to find the image with which some group can identify. This was the brilliance of the Charlie (fragrance) image. It appealed *at the time* to a segment of the female population that identified with the lifestyle of a liberated, active, competent woman stepping out to be successful.

Any fashion is adopted only to a degree since not everyone's physical and personality characteristics fit the new fashion; the miniskirt was not the immediate favorite of older women. However, those not fitting the fashion usually still want to signal they are aware of it by making an occasional fashionable purchase.

Fads

Although the words "fad" and "fashion" are often used synonymously, they can be distinguished. Fads are short-lived and noncyclical. They are adopted with a more intense and exaggerated zeal than fashion. They can amount to a "craze" for just about any product that excites curiosity and offers the potential for the consumer to be part of an in-group. The hula hoop is a classic example. It was a craze that excited curiosity and gave rise to in-groups based on members having mastered the technique of hula hooping.

Fads provoke curiosity by being new, different, and offering the promise of excitement. They are short-lived because curiosity is quickly satisfied and the promise of excitement does not live up to expectations. Fads tend to "catch on" among the young since it is the young who seek novelty and identity with the in-group and its bandwagon. The manufacturer's problem lies in predicting what will catch on and whether the fad's short existence justifies its manufacture and promotion.

Status and Power

In adhering to convention, fashion, or faddish pursuits, consumers are acting as if following instructions or rules for conforming to peer group expectations. Such conformity may or may not confer status or power. Yet people generally desire high status and power relative to those with whom they mix providing they can attain that status and power without endangering their group membership.

More significantly for our purposes, people want to signal their status in society by possessions. Among the relatively affluent working class there is always a demand for goods that unambiguously signal status within their social class. Examples are designer clothes, leather jackets, top-price motorcycles, oversized portable stereos, and so on. It is not just the "vulgar rich" who indulge in competitive display! It is all too easy to identify the working class as always belonging to the lowest price segment of a market, even though this is not necessarily so. For example, the manufacturer of the most expensive ready-made suit in Europe discovered that many of their regular customers were coal miners and other well-paid blue collar workers. In large, anonymous urban communities material possessions often come to be a gauge of status.

Advertising and Status

Advertising has traditionally exploited the fear of being lost in the crowd by holding out the possibility of status or equality with the rich and famous by encouraging the fantasy that this can all be achieved by using the same brand of lipstick or whatever as those at the top.

Although a brand that is known to be expensive may be bought as a status symbol, services known to be offered only to carefully selected clients can confer even more status. Thus, the London banking firm of C. Hoare & Co. will only consider someone as a new customer if they have been recommended by a long-time client and passed a personal interview. Hoare has never been short of clients.

Although certain products may be sought as emblems of status, they may also be a source of power for boosting the ego or sense of worth. In service industries, personal recognition of customers and clients is such a boost to self-esteem that it constitutes a major factor in customer satisfaction with the service. Power itself implies the ability to influence others in a direction favored by the power holder. For example, in some relationships a superior education bestows power. Whenever certain goods (e.g., property) increase the dependency of others (e.g., tenants), such goods provide power to the owners. Perhaps even dressing sexily or being beautiful is a potential source of power.

Sometimes the symbol of power (e.g., a title in Britain) may mean little in real terms, but may still be highly prized (as evidenced by the prices paid for titles when Lloyd George was discreetly selling them off), as many will take the symbol to be the substance of power. Power always attracts respectful followers.

Brand Name "Snob Appeal"

Whereas brand names do not necessarily carry over their image to products outside some obvious family of products, a brand name that has snob appeal can generate demand for a wide range of products with no family resemblance beyond the name. Do people really believe that the Tiffany or Cartier name on a watch ensures better technical performance than the name Timex? People pay for the name,—not for its guarantee of excellence but for its snob appeal. What else could lead people to pay enormous prices for plastic handbags and luggage of undistinguished design which scream out an expensive designer name?

Firms are not always candid when they promote snob appeal. Thus, London Fog still sets its advertisements in London—which suggests that their product is an import from England—when their raincoats are actually made in Baltimore, Maryland.

Image Advertising

Sometimes the illusion of status coupled with a sense of community with others can arise from purchases associated with celebrities. Consumers who visibly identify in some way with a celebrity (for example by wearing jeans with a Calvin Klein label) signal their values to the world and share a sense of community with those making the same identification. But everything depends on whether buying the product promoted by the celebrity will, in fact, be perceived by the consumer as signalling such values. The product and the celebrity must be perceived as having the appropriate affinity.

Consumers identify with both celebrities and the images of a lifestyle promoted by advertising. Distinguishing a brand on the basis of image may swing a sale and convert a consumer from what would otherwise be a picking situation. This is true of many products seemingly bought purely on the basis of taste, such as beer and cigarettes. Advertisers are always on the look-out for historic symbols or current celebrities with which to associate the advertised brand to enhance its image. If nothing else comes to mind, there is always sex as a standby—a beautiful woman in a bathing suit has been used even to sell coffins!

A frequent criticism of such image advertising is that it bypasses reason in that there is no argument but only a loose collection of images and ideas (Nolt, 1984). The cowboy of the Marlboro cigarette advertisement is typical of image advertising. So is the slogan for Virginia Slims cigarettes, "You've come a long way, baby," shown against a background picture of a turn-of-the-century woman contrasted with the modern emancipated woman smoking a cigarette. The aim is to promote the idea that full emancipation from men is associated with smoking Virginia Slims. Although it is true that advertisements such as these do not dwell on tangible product attributes, they do provide social reasons for buying—even if such reasons are not regarded as substantive by others. On the other hand, image advertising is commonly used when a brand would be otherwise undistin-guished. This is particularly so if under image advertising we include advertisements showing admired personalities using the brand.

Integrity

In a sense, buying actions are always acts of self-expression in that they embody the consumer's own goals and wants and express how consumers define themselves. Buying is particularly self-expressive when influenced by the buyer's own sense of per-sonal integrity.

People have perceptions of themselves as moral agents, and the buying decision can reflect their moral ideals to "generate the experience of helping to bring these things (ideals) within reach even if an illusion," (Schick, 1984). Consumers do not always choose to maximize personal returns. They may forego self-interest to follow what they believe is right, for example,

Investors may forego lucrative opportunities in South Africa for the sake of their ideals.

Consumers may not follow fashion if it involves furs, skins, or cosmetics that come from the slaughter of animals.

Consumers may feel the need to support domestic industries, unionized firms, and firms with a reputation for advancing the ideals of which the consumer approves.

As Nestlé found when it failed to respond adequately to the criticisms of its baby food promotions in the Third World, consumers can boycott firms they consider to be in breach of accepted standards of ethical conduct.

There are those who would deny that any altruistic motives operate in buying. Sociology's exchange theory, for example, assumes that people are motivated exclusively by self-interest. But some buying actions manifestly lead to a loss in personal welfare. Although an economist may argue that the individual consumer is still maximizing utility in the sense that any material losses from not investing in South Africa, for example, are more than compensated by the satisfaction stemming from a sense of moral righteousness. But this rests on defining utility as whatever it is the consumer seeks to maximize, in which case buying action will be viewed as always maximizing utility as a matter of definition.

ADAPTIVE CRITERIA

There is always some uncertainty in buying. Adaptive criteria are the rules used to cope with this uncertainty and with any information overload about the costs and benefits of rival brands. Even if everything were known about a product or a set of rival brands, there would always be consumer uncertainty as to future preferences (March 1978). However, some uncertainty is not perceived as a practical uncertainty and, as in habit, consumers may unhesitatingly make their choice.

The increasing proliferation of brands and the increasing complexity of many products make for consumer confusion and uncertainty. The degree to which consumers are concerned about this uncertainty depends on the importance of the purchase, the sacrifices of money and effort involved, and the anticipated loss of self-esteem that results from recognizing they have made a mistake.

In the marketing literature, the same view is expressed when risk is defined as the product of uncertainty and the possible consequences associated with the product. But becoming knowledgeable about all the relevant products and/or brands is both not feasible and too expensive in terms of time, money, and frustration. Consumers seldom even need exhaustive knowledge about rival brands. Consumers need only search for enough information to determine a preference. Yet we would expect the greater the uncertainty and the more important the decision, the greater the search for information (Jacoby, Chestnut, Fisher, 1978). Under high-perceived risk conditions it is not surprising to find a tendency to consult both personal sources (i.e., friends) and neutral sources (e.g., consumer reports) (Locander and Hermann, 1979).

Reducing uncertainty means reducing the possibility of making a mistake. We all seek to avoid the emotional discomfort associated with decisions we regret. (Bell, 1982, 1985). There is a lust for absolute certainty among consumers so that even practical certainty is discounted. Few consumers can accept the idea of being completely uncertain. However, some consumers are more disposed than others to the use of adaptive criteria. As expected, decisions matter more and uncertainties are likely to be higher among the poor. Sometimes they have more restricted access to information; other times they are unable to cope with the information overload. It is also unsurprising that it is middle and upper class consumers who are more likely to seek information, particularly from independent sources (Foxall, 1975).

The desire to avoid error is one explanation for habitually buying the same brand since this involves fewer surprises. Consumers may be prepared to sacrifice the advantage of having the latest product for reduced risk. This is one of the reasons consumers are reluctant to switch to the new brands entering the market without a strong incentive to do so. It is common for the marketing literature to speak of risk-averters who act to minimize risk and risk-seekers who show a preference for risk. However, because consumers seem prepared to take abnormal risks does not demonstrate a preference for it when buying. They may simply have different beliefs about the risks involved and differ in the strength of their desires.

In applying adaptive criteria the consumer acts as if employing one or more of the rules below:

Imitation: Follow what others do who are known to be knowledgeable.

Advice: Turn to people you can trust.

Brand Image or Reputation: Keep to the firms or brands you can trust.

Sample or Comparison Shopping: Turn to the experience you can trust.

Warranties and Guarantees: Insure your trust.

A consumer may habitually follow the same rule for coping with uncertainty and information overload. For example, a consumer may always feel the need to seek advice or imitate those assumed to be "in the know."

When consumers buy a product for the first time, they may consider all the brands to be equally risky buys, so that the degree of risk attached to each alternative may not discriminate between them. However, although this may be the initial position, the opportunities for risk reduction are likely to differ among the brands along with the opportunity for applying adaptive criteria.

Imitation

The consumer may be bewildered by the many brands from which to choose. Sometimes, consumers seek to avoid such bewilderment by giving up some of their freedom to choose by leaving the choice to others. In *imitating* others, the consumer resolves any practical uncertainty by buying the same brand as someone considered to be in the know—someone who through position, reputation, or access to relevant information sources can be more or less guaranteed to choose wisely (Sheth 1968). In the absence of any such figure, the consumer may choose the most popular brand on the ground that the collective judgment is unlikely to lead to serious error (Roselius 1971). This is one reason the well-established brand is difficult to displace—new entrants are by definition not the market leaders. The established leader acquires a legitimacy through long tenure which is unlikely to be seriously undermined by minor advantages offered by some johnny-come-lately.

Imitative behavior arises not only from a desire to socially conform but also from a conviction that copying others in the know is one way of avoiding error. However, following the choices of some individual is a rule of limited application since there may be no one to imitate.

Advice

Advice is frequently sought when a product is complex, when several brands are perceived as having significant relevant differences, and when the product is socially visible. Advice that warns against buying some particular brand is more likely to be accepted than advice that recommends. This is because risk avoidance is more likely to be paramount. Even if advice is not decisive, there is satisfaction in knowing that someone else has approved the choice. Independent advice generally has more of an impact, (Newman and Staelin 1973), for example,

> I knew I would get a true answer from Jim who already owns a Mercedes and knows what I'm after, than from a report, salesman, or advertisement.

But nonindependent advice is frequently consulted.

> I sought advice first from the top stores since they tend to give more and better advice. Advice from a discount store is not to be trusted even though I might later buy there once I know which brand to buy.

Advice is frequently sought to confirm tentative choices or to seek confirmation of one's own thinking. Thus, husbands and wives may turn to each other seemingly for advice when both partners know they are really seeking support for a particular purchase.

Advertising often takes on the role of adviser by employing a celebrity or some credible and attractive figure to put across "facts" about the product. Imitating the preferences of others and/or seeking advice are common tactics where technical performance is of acute concern, for example,

- Consumer durables that are infrequently bought, such as washing machines, hi-fi equipment, sports equipment, and so on.
- Investment and other services that are to be performed in the future, for example, travel services.
- Consumer nondurables whose performance is difficult to assess from inspection yet important to know, as in the case of health products.
- High-priced purchases whose benefits cannot be gauged by inspection.

Where there is a proliferation of brands, consumers are confused as to which brands to choose. For example, it is nearly impossible to test each of the approximately 172 brands of fragrance on the market. Even in choosing a coffee percolator one customer in a protocol said:

> My mind boggled at the huge variety of choice and huge price range. I was quite bewildered and had no idea which to choose.

Or, as another respondent said about choosing a telephone answering machine,

> They had about 25 different kinds and they all looked the same. It was terribly confusing to me but much too serious to just choose randomly.

(Both consumers first used the conjunctive rule described in Chapter 8.)

Brand Image/Reputation

Where choice is very individual and price is of minor importance, seeking advice may seem socially inappropriate. In such circumstances, *brand image/reputation* may be crucial since familiarity can be the key. The consumer resolves to buy a name brand in the belief that this offers some assurance. Thus, consumers may not know how to judge the optical qualities of sunglasses, but they believe that a famous manufacturer would never risk the firm's reputation by producing a poor technical product. Hence, the consumer may infer quality from the brand name. The choice may also be based on country of origin, for example, Japanese tape-recorders, English china, French wine, Swiss watches, Italian handbags, or German engineering.

Consumers may reject a brand because it is unknown, for example,

> I have never heard of the brand—I'd have heard of them if they were that good.

Or the choice may be based largely on the brand name, for example,

> You can't go wrong buying IBM.

Designer fashion has the double advantage of appealing to the desire to be fashionable while additionally making the brand familiar by association with a well-known designer. For many consumers, this reduces both uncertainty as to social appropriateness and uncertainty about quality.

Advertising frequently seeks to reassure the consumer about the trustworthiness of a brand, for example,

"You can be sure if it's a Westinghouse."
"State Farm is all you need to know about insurance."
"With a name like Smuckers it has to be good."
"Cadbury means quality."

Familiarity in itself reduces uncertainty since being familiar suggests being well-known and being well-known suggests having stood the test of time and public scrutiny. Hence the importance of developing familiarity in advertising, for example,

> We remembered having seen ads for "Jennifer Convertibles" on buses and in subways. These ads had pictures and prices that seemed reasonable so we decided to visit Jennifer Convertibles first.

Of course, it may not be the reputation of the brand but the reputation of the store that is all-important, for example,

> I don't know about whether some of the other stores are trustworthy, but I knew 47th St. Photo was a reputable place.

Where there are no concrete bases for choice, a brand with a credible and attractive image wins out. Both the credibility and attractiveness of whatever or whoever is putting across information lower the defenses of the consumer. A credible source is convincing because what is signaled coheres with existing beliefs, while an attractive source is persuasive because the message is in some way supportive of the consumer's self-image. Just as we judge the credibility of strangers on the basis of their appearance, the claims they make and the way they field questions, so consumers must sometimes judge brands on the basis of their packaging, claims made, and how well advertising and labeling address consumer uncertainties. Again, just as an open and friendly stranger is attractive and conjures up the image of an ideal friend, we identify with product images with which we are comfortable. Products with attractive images seem to reduce uncertainty. As the head of a brewery once said, "Our business is not just making beer. No, making friends is our business." In other words, attractiveness helps credibility.

Just as a sense of humor can add to the attractiveness of those we meet, so humor in advertising can add to an attractive image. Humor can disarm defenses. However, a humorous tone may conflict with a serious one, so the serious information aspect of a message (if any were intended) may be lost. Hence, humor can be destructive if there is a serious job of education to be done. Also, hearing the same joke every night can get a bit thin!

Sample or Comparison Shopping

In the face of high-cost decisions the rational consumer is typically viewed as undertaking extensive shopping to collect information to resolve factual uncertainty. Certainly, *comparison shopping* does occur to find out about prices and what is available but is probably less common than supposed (Katona and Mueller, 1954). As one consumer said: "I always thought I'd do a lot of research before making a major purchase, but there is never time." This consumer might have added that consumers do not generally have the inclination to undertake an extensive amount of learning: it means hard mental effort during which consumption is postponed and gratification delayed.

Where appropriate, a *sample* or *trial offer* can turn a doubter into a believer. Although there may still be uncertainty as to whether the sampled product is the best buy for them, consumers at least know what to expect. In the nineteenth century, J. B. Stetson got sales of his famous hat off the ground by sending to every major hat dealer in the Southwest a sample of the hat together with an accompanying order form. Similarly, the basis of Estee Lauder's success in fragrances was through the offer of samples.

Consumers, it is assumed, learn by trial and error. This is true only if they are willing to engage in trials and the situation allows learning from experience. Neither assumption may be true at the time of purchase. As one consumer commented about buying a videocassette recorder:

> I can't reach a decision now on which of these models to buy. I don't understand any of the technicalities, and the prices vary enormously for seemingly minor differences. How do I judge which of them is even likely to be the most reliable?

Trying out several brands (even when the financial cost is low and the frequency of purchase high) always risks disappointment and the emotional reaction of having made an error. Experience, too, is not always decisive since results are often vague or even ambiguous (for example, use of a hair conditioner) leaving much room for conjecture. Under such conditions, beliefs may fall in line with the presuppositions generated by advertising.

Warranties and Guarantees

Where there are risks in respect to the product's reliability and performance, warranties and guarantees have the potential to provide reassurance and trigger the sale. But consumers have come to be suspicious of many warranties and guarantees. The best guarantees are the "money back if not satisfied" made by a reputable dealer or where such a dealer undertakes to put right *immediately* or replace anything as soon as it goes wrong.

ECONOMIC CRITERIA

Economic criteria are concerned with the outlays of money, time, and effort that have to be spent in buying, using, or consuming a product. Such outlays are set against the perceived benefits of the product or brand. In this sense, not buying is rewarding as economic sacrifice is avoided. That a cost avoided is a form of self-reward is reflected in how frequently consumers compliment themselves on not having bought something. The seller's problem lies in establishing the point at which enough consumers will perceive the critical advantage of the offering as greater than the sacrifice involved.

Benefits Versus Sacrifice

Usually consumers have to be attracted to a new product before considering price. However, once a consumer's interest is aroused, interest shifts to what must be given up in return. Reaction to price (e.g., whether it is judged reasonable) is very much influenced by the extent to which interest in the product has already been aroused. The initial focus of any seller who is intent on attracting new buyers should be on "selling" what the product can do—even though consumers may decide not to buy when they know the price.

The consumer implicitly ranks alternative products on the

basis of the sacrifices likely to be involved. When such an ordering occurs, the immediate consequences of making a purchase are known. These consequences may constitute a reason for *not* going ahead. Purchase indecision may arise when consumers are unsure of the future consequences of the purchase. After all, future circumstances (and hence future preferences) cannot always be predicted and the product itself may be vague in what it promises.

Reaction to High Prices

In the case of frequently bought products, consumers do not always check prices and are often ignorant of price. This can be misleading, however, if it is taken as suggesting consumers attach little weight to price. Lack of attention to price may simply indicate confidence that prices at the store are competitive and price differences among brands remain roughly as before.

High prices always exclude some consumers from purchase, but they can also be an attraction. A high price can be what makes a highly visible luxury product attractive by suggesting exclusivity. Thus, one brand of perfume entered the market making no promises whatever, being simply advertised as the most expensive perfume in the world. At the height of the cutthroat price competition among U.S. domestic airlines, one airline charging full fare simply promoted the satisfaction engendered by passengers knowing their neighbors on the flight would also be full fare passengers! Currently, there is a watch being advertised at $4,400 which makes no claim about the watch's performance but simply that it is the thinnest watch in the world. Where price does however inhibit purchase, sellers need to focus on depreciating the sacrifice (e.g., "this is an investment, not a payment") while clarifying any dubious benefits.

Consumer hesitation in paying the price demanded for some products may reflect a habitual disposition or attitude toward such a purchase, for example, "I have a certain resistance to buying jewelry. It always seems a rather frivolous, extravagant purchase." In such situations, advertising needs to give the consumer an excuse to follow his or her basic inclinations (e.g., "Treat yourself; you deserve the best"). Where integrative criteria are not important, designer label brands may even be rejected out of hand as indicative of "paying through the nose."

Where competing brands are sold at the same price (as, for example, with many bank services), price cannot be a discriminator. However, this is the exception.

In general, consumers implicitly categorize brands into price categories and expect brands falling within the same price range to offer roughly the same value but not necessarily the same set of benefits. The seller can and should facilitate such categorizing by justifying price differences in a way that is meaningful to the consumer.

Reaction to Low Prices

Perceptions as to the reasonableness of price are all important. If the price appears abnormally low, there are suspicions about quality. If the price is abnormally high, there is a suspicion about the extra value being given for the extra cost. The importance attached to prices within a quality level depends on what experience has taught about prices. As one woman shopper worded it, "Since New York stores are always having sales, it is essential to compare prices."

A low price can lead to a passive want for a product if suspicions are not removed. On occasion, suspicions may be removed by showing the country of origin, naming of the manufacturer, or emphasizing the low price as a special promotion. Sales are often perceived as an opportunity for a bargain which (since bargains are scarce) are also seen as something which should be seized while the going is good. Slogans such as "special offer," "last chance," "going out of business," and so on are meant to trigger buying by their suggestion of future regret if the opportunity is not seized. Seizing opportunities possesses the appeal of providing instant gratification, avoiding future regret, and enhancing confidence in doing well. If the seller can get the consumer to perceive a product as a bargain, there is perhaps nothing so effective at triggering sales. But even in a sale the price may still arouse suspicion. As one respondent said

> Because it was selling for a quarter of its original price I felt there must be something wrong with the model.

What of the manufacturer who seeks to dominate the market by selling at the lowest price? On occasion, with certain product categories, there is just no way to dominate a market by price.

High fashion, for example, is never fashionable if it is cheap. Products bought to be in fashion, mark occasions, signal status, and so on are not likely to be the cheapest brands. As one buyer worded it,

> I want a high quality gin for the occasion so I'm eliminating domestic brands entirely as they are so cheap.

Paying for the best and desiring to avoid acknowledging an error disposes consumers to a favorable evaluation when they are initially convinced they have bought the best. Some consumers act as if they believe in the universal validity of price and quality going together or, at least, use it as a working rule to save time and trouble. Such consumers are not disposed to consider the low-priced brand at all. However, this rejection of the lowest price does not necessarily mean consumers believe the low-priced brand disproportionately sacrifices quality for price. They may want to reduce risk or, because social factors also influence buying, they are often willing to pay more.

Price, Quality, and Perceived Value for Money

Consumers are frequently unsure about quality or knowing whether extra benefits are worth the extra price. For example, what attributes do you use to measure the quality of the items in this list:

Toothpaste	Lipstick
Cigarettes	Beer
Shampoo	Wristwatch
Leather shoes	TV set
Car tires	Laundry detergent
Gasoline	Headache remedy
Cereal	Pet food
Coffee	Bread
Jeans	

Sometimes price itself may be used as the indicator of quality. As one respondent said:

> However, there are different qualities of wool and a variety of weaves and it is really most difficult for the ordinary shopper to judge the quality of a carpet except by price.

A manufacturer (e.g., Ford with its Model T) may dominate a market through low price. But in the absence of a large, pent-up, passive demand being inhibited by price or easily recognizable value for money (as was the case with many Japanese products), firms might find it more profitable not to be the cheapest but to be perceived as best value for money. When the price is but a small part of the total cost of the event (e.g., the price of a wedding cake), or performance in the function is critical (e.g., razor blades), then the higher-priced brands will attract buyers if price and quality are believed to be related. But in a mature market where products are essentially the same, price can be critical.

Consumers who are worried about quality are disposed to buy at a premium price to avoid making an error. Also, where performance in the function envisaged for a product is of key importance, consumers may be prepared to pay a premium price when the relationship between price and performance is unknown. As one buyer of cosmetics worded it:

> I wanted to believe that you could pay more to get better results and if I'd had to pay $100, I would have.

To this buyer, looking better was such a key goal that price, within limits, was not significant. However, consumers often act as they do in social encounters: they hate to be outwitted and lose self-esteem. Just as a failure to achieve a job promotion is perceived as less of a loss than a demotion, consumers are generally more concerned with avoiding a loss than making an equivalent gain. For instance, consumers do not generally hire services without some knowledge of cost. They may, in fact, turn down some services—even if the service is objectively worth much more to them—if they believe the price cheats them of 20 cents. Consumers resent pricing that suggests putting one over on them. For example, the practice of quoting a price for an "all inclusive" package suggests no hidden cost surprises, and is appealing. But consumers have a sense of losing out when prices are raised after a price promotion, and they may be hesitant about rebuying. (Most price promotions, however, simply "rent" allegiance for the duration of the campaign.)

Consumers are anxious to know what they are letting themselves in for. Unless this is made clear, the want for the product or brand may remain passive. The demand for medical, dental, legal, and other services is dampened by uncertainty about what it will all cost. Contrary to the expressed fears of professional associations, the publication of fees is unlikely to lead to any price wars—but would certainly lead to more business. The professional organizations themselves probably believe this. What they really resent is the symbolic nature of price lists— how awful it would be to think you value your time less than some co-professional nearby!

Price Maximum

The maximum price that can be obtained by the seller depends on the consumer's dependency on the individual manufacturer's brand rather than the importance of the product. If the consumer believes that what the brand has to offer is of central importance to the functions for which the product is being bought and yet is unique to the brand, the consumer is highly dependent on the seller and the seller is in a position to charge a premium price. However, if the price is believed to be extortionate, there can be no satisfied customer; only temporary allegiance until the customer finds an alternative.

With a drop in real income, each unit of income becomes that much more valuable and sensitivity to price becomes that more acute. Consider, for example, the swing to generic products during a time of inflation. But, not so obviously, there is a more determined search for value for money when the economy is suffering from both inflation and depression. With inflation there is a wish to buy today (in case money buys less tomorrow) at yesterday's prices but a depression also kindles the desire to guard against an uncertain future by investing in products that will last.

Additional Economic Criteria

Economic criteria embrace not only the price paid but also anticipated operating costs, repair costs, and so on, as well as the time and effort generated by the purchase. For example, neither intrinsic preference nor nutritional value is the sole basis for a choice of food. Speed and ease of preparation have become important. Just making a convenient purchase at the point of sale can add to sales. This was recognized long ago when a Lifesaver Candy salesman told the retailer to "Just put a few near the cash register with the price tag and then be sure every customer gets a nickel with his change and see what happens."

Although costs other than price may lead a consumer to forego purchase, consumers may dismiss the cost of shopping around for lower prices. Because of the emotional overtones of not letting the other fellow get away with anything consumers may not rationally calculate the cost of comparison shopping.

USE FUNCTIONS, GENERATED FUNCTIONS, AND COMPETITION

In thinking about competition it is necessary to think about use functions, generated functions, and intrinsic appeal. The extent to which brands perform the same core use functions with equal efficiency is the extent to which the brands are substitutes for each other. But the extent to which such substitutes are close segment rivals depends on (1) whether ancillary and convenience-in-use functions overlap *and* (2) the extent to which the brands have the same intrinsic appeal and meet the same generated functions as reflected in integrative, economic, and adaptive criteria. For instance, a Rolex watch and a Timex watch could possibly be regarded as substitutes since both serve the same core use function of measuring time. But they are not in direct competition since Rolex and Timex are wide apart in the economic, integrative, adaptive, and perhaps even the intrinsic preference criteria to which they appeal.

SUMMARY

This chapter discussed the application by the consumer of choice criteria that relate to integrative, adaptive, and economy functions.

The pursuit of *integrative functions* reflect the consumer's concern with social opinion, status, self-image, and the preservation of personal integrity. Integrative choice criteria are influenced by:

- *Convention*. Consumers are socialized into adopting the conventions of their particular social milieu because following convention helps in predicting behavior so individual efforts can be coordinated.
- *Fashion*. What is currently fashionable in the consumers' social milieu is likely to influence buying. Fashion in clothes, for example, allows the consumer to slip into a new identity to incite the interest, envy, admiration, and approval of others.
- *Fads*. Fads are adopted when they offer novelty, the promise of excitement, and belonging to some in-group if some technique, knowledge, or ritual associated with the fad is mastered.
- *Status*. Through their possessions, people can signal their current status or the status to which they aspire.
- *Power*. Some products, such as education, ownership of large

amounts of real estate, and other highly visible forms of wealth are sources of not only status but also of power.

- *Personal integrity*. Consumer buying actions can reflect moral ideals to generate the experience of helping to bring these ideals into reach.

Adaptive functions are considered whenever the consumer uses choice criteria that reflect the consumer's concern with uncertainty and information overload. Adaptive strategies for coping with uncertainty are:

- Habitually buying the same brand.
- Imitating the buying choices of those considered "in the know."
- Taking advice about what brand to buy, what to look for in judging quality, and so on.
- Choosing the brand with the best reputation or from a firm or country that has the best reputation in the field.

Economy functions are considered whenever the consumer uses choice criteria that reflect concern with what has to be given up to secure the benefits of a product. Several generalizations can be made.

- The reaction to the price of a new product is influenced in part by the extent to which interest in the product has been aroused.
- A low price can lead to a passive want for a product unless suspicions about the low price are removed. Where integrative functions are important to a consumer, the lowest-priced brand may in fact be rejected. Also when consumers find it difficult to judge quality, price may be used as an indicator of quality.
- Consumers are concerned with not losing out in any market exchange. Anything in pricing that suggests putting one over on the consumer, such as hidden costs, will be resented.
- The maximum price chargeable relates to:

  The importance the customer attaches to the functions for which the product is being bought.

  The centrality of the firm's brand for the performance of those functions.

  Whether the brand's benefits are unique to the firm.

- Economy functions embrace not only price but other costs. A firm can develop a critical advantage by demonstrating that their brand reduces these other costs.

IMPLICATIONS FOR MARKETING

1. If the firm's product is socially visible, the firm should identify and try to enhance the *integrative functions* served by the product, namely,

    (a) Conventions in the consumer's social milieu.
    (b) Fashion in the consumer's social milieu.
    (c) Status/esteem/respect in the consumer's social milieu.
    (d) Power in the consumer's social milieu.
    (e) Obligations reflecting the consumer's ideals as to personal integrity.

2. Where consumer choice appears to be simply a matter of liking (intrinsic preference), and brands are all equally liked, the firm increases brand worth to the consumer by demonstrating the brand also serves integrative functions. Different brands symbolize different degrees of adherence to convention and fashion or reflect different degrees of status or conformity to values.

3. Where consumers are concerned that products do not violate personal norms of integrity, the firm may identify a gap in the market by catering more explicitly to such ideals.

4. Where consumers are likely to lack substantive knowledge about the relative merits of rival offerings, the firm should develop persuasive communications that exploit knowledge of the strategies adopted by consumers when applying adaptive criteria.

Consumer Strategy	Possible Company Action
Imitate those "in the know"	Show those "in the know" buy the brand or point out the brand is the market leader.
Advice sought	Encourage existing buyers to recommend the brand.
Reputation considered	Establish an image of credibility and attractiveness or being well-known.
Sampling	Provide samples, trial offers, or other ways of allowing the consumer to have direct experience with the brand at minimum risk.
Comparison shopping	Develop a push strategy at the point-of-sale.

5. In selling a new product the firm should draw attention first to getting the prospect "sold" on the benefits of their offering so that the consumer applies economic criteria after being stimulated to desire the product.

6. If the firm's product is a high quality product, a high price reinforces the quality image and should be adopted.

7. If an image of exclusivity is sought, a relatively very high price can reinforce the image.

8. The firm should identify consumer perceptions of the value of its brand relative to rival offerings as consumers expect brands falling within the same value range to be roughly the same price.

9. Whenever a firm charges more than its competitors for its product, the firm must signal value differences equivalent to the price difference.

10. Where the firm is using price as a competitive strategy, the firm should reinforce the strategy by demonstrating or suggesting the product is a bargain. Providing the firm's brand is perceived as a quality product in terms of key functions, many consumers will trade off much else for a lower relative price.

11. As consumers budget their time as well as their money and seek to "spend" it wisely, firms should seek to minimize this cost or sacrifice as this enhances the value of their offering.

12. The brands perceived by the consumer as offering the same intrinsic appeal, integrative, technical, adaptive, and economy functions are those brands which are perceived as being most in competition with each other.

Comment on Protocol Statement for Purchase of Personal Computer

1. GOAL(S)

   i. *Organizational:* To increase the efficiency of operations and to increase sales.

   ii. *Normative:* To be knowledgeable rather than ignorant.

   iii. *Aspiration level:* To signal to others an image of a progressive businessman and to keep abreast of relevant business technology.

2. WANT(S)

The buyer had initially a passive want for a computer but was inhibited by

   i. The fear of not being able to use and master a computer.

   ii. The potential cost of a computer.

The passive want was aroused by a commercial showing people just walking right off the street to discuss computers in Computerland Stores. The buyer's interest was sustained by the salesman's

   (a) Credibility/perceived competence

   (b) Attractiveness

   (c) Claims as to the benefits of employing a computer

      —Handling accounts receivable, accounts payable, and the general ledger

      —More up-to-date information

      —Money saved from tighter control of accounts

      —Increased sales from tighter control of inventory to avoid stockouts and mailings to regular customers to let them know about sales

      —Cash flow projections and sales forecasting

      —Word processing

Although the buyer became convinced about the potential benefits of the computer for his business, this did not in itself activate the passive want. This was because the salesman still needed to deal with the doubts and objections of the buyer, namely,

    (a) Fear of being unable to use the computer

    (b) Potential cost of a computer system

How these inhibitions were overcome is discussed below under the heading "adaptive criteria."

3. BELIEFS

   i. The buyer's primary interest in buying a computer rested on the belief that a computer could help his business. This belief was supportive of buying and reinforced after talking to the salesman.

  ii. The buyer lacked computer skills and perhaps the aptitude for using a computer. This belief inhibited buying.

 iii. Choosing the right computer was very important because of the potential economic repercussions. This belief inhibited buying.

4. CHOICE CRITERIA

Technical Functions

   i. *Core use function:* The buyer assumed both the IBM PC and Apple IIe would be able to carry out the functions described by the salesman in listing potential benefits. However, the buyer inferred the superiority of the IBM PC from its appearance of sturdiness: it was solid looking and felt solid when compared with the Apple. Also, the PC keyboard, unlike the Apple keyboard, made a clicking sound when the buyer hit the keys so the user would know if the key was hit hard enough.

  ii. *Ancillary use functions:* Perhaps a suspicion is entertained by the buyer that the IBM PC would have the widest possible scope. This would be consistent with the buyer's bias toward the IBM PC (as the buyer's selective perception indicates).

 iii. *Convenience-in-use functions:* The IBM PC was again preferred as the keyboard was maneuverable while the Apple's keyboard was physically attached to the computer.

Integrative Functions

Integrative criteria played an important role in disposing the buyer toward buying:

(a) With the whole world becoming interested in computers and the buyer didn't want to be left out.
(b) The computer is a status symbol; computer mailings would also make the buyer appear more progressive and professional.

Economy Functions

The buyer was initially worried by potential costs but once this problem was cleared up economic criteria did not play an important role in either choosing a computer or in choosing the IBM. Initially $6,000 to $7,000 price range was the order of magnitude suggested by others to the buyer. On being informed of possible cost saving and tax allowances, the buyer was prepared to consider use-value in deciding his reservation price. Also, the tax break made the difference in price between the IBM PC and the Apple appear unimportant to the buyer.

Adaptive Functions

Adaptive criteria were key throughout the buying process and were the most important factors in deciding between the IBM PC and the Apple. The buyer was fearful of not being competent enough to master a computer and of being saddled with many hidden costs. Such fears were reinforced by stories of firms never being able to get their computers to perform satisfactorily. Added to such fears was information overload.

The factors involved in adaptive criteria that led the buyer to favor the IBM PC were

i. The fact that in buying the IBM brand the buyer would be imitating those judged to be "in the know" like friends and associates who had bought the IBM PC including the salesman himself. IBM was also known to be the best seller.
ii. Advice from associates, friends and the salesman.
iii. The reputation of IBM. The reputation of IBM suggested it was more likely to be around in the future to give a continuity of service. The buyer believed that brand name was important and rejected the Televideo brand simply on the ground of not having heard of it.
iv. The greater familiarity with IBM. The buyer had been satisfied with other IBM products and its service while finding the IBM's Charlie Chaplin commercial very reassuring.
v. The IBM warranty and service contract.

The buyer was predisposed to buy the IBM and simply went through the motions of considering the Apple. Even at the most superficial level the evaluation of the IBM PC in terms of adaptive criteria gave it a considerable edge over the Apple computer. However, the decision to buy a computer at all resulted from the way the salesman met the buyer's adaptive choice criteria.

    (a) The salesman narrowed the range of alternatives considered by the buyer. The buyer had wanted him to do this.

    (b) The salesman's credibility and attractiveness reassured the buyer that a computer could perform the functions envisaged for it by the buyer.

    (c) The salesman removed the buyer's worry about not being able to master the computer by
       —Explaining how things worked
       —Demonstrating relevant software
       —Showing the buyer that using the computer could be enjoyable
       —Offering two free classes.

Intrinsic Appeal

The buyer showed a preference for IBM's sleek design while IBM in its commercials projected an image with which the buyer could identify.

Decision Making

We suspect the buyer had an initial disposition that favored buying the IBM PC and this biased perceptions of the Apple IIe. However, such a bias would be easier to recognize if the buyer's "thinking aloud" had been recorded simultaneously with the actual buying process.

Implications for Marketing

If this businessman was representative of other proprietors of small businesses contemplating buying a computer, there are certain marketing implications. In general, prospective buyers are held back from buying by uncertainty as to whether they will be able to master the computer and whether the computer will perform as expected. Such uncertainty is characteristic of any new market for a consumer durable in the early stages of growth. Such uncertainty suggests the marketing strategy should focus on:

    i. Offering training
   ii. Showing ease of operation
  iii. Stressing the firm's reputation
  iv. Offering of technical assistance

—Presales service
—Installation
—Postsales service to ensure the computer lives up to expectations
  v. Taking the prospect to see successful applications

1. Product
   As the buyer judges core use function by sturdy, solid appearance, the computer should project such attributes and avoid an image of cheapness.
   Convenience-in-use (down to pressing the keys!) should be a major thrust when considering potential product improvements since ease of use reduces uncertainty about mastering the computer. A competitive edge over the competition with respect to the ease of learning how to use the computer could be a critical advantage.

2. Promotion
   Promotional appeals should focus on reducing uncertainty by minimizing (in line with the Charlie Chaplin commercial) the learning problem and stressing that an overall price could be given.

3. Price
   Buyers are prepared to pay a premium price to lessen risk.

4. Distribution and Service
   Whether the firm sells direct or through distributors, sales people are key in both getting prospects sold on what the computer can do for them and in getting them moving toward buying. Any company sales person or distributor who offers to:
   i. Solve the buyer's application problems.
   ii. Specify the whole computer/software system that will be needed to meet the buyer's needs.
   iii. Train the buyer to run the system
   iv. Provide an all-inclusive price for an offering that fully meets the buyer's requirements
will have a critical advantage. The firm that makes the first move in offering such a total systems package is likely to have a sustainable critical advantage since accumulated experience will count. However, the problem does not lie in judging the desirability from the customer's point of view of doing these things. The problem lies in judging the feasibility and commercial viability of doing these things.

8

Deliberation, Preference, Buying Intentions, and Post-Purchase Satisfaction

Rationality in buying and the biases that result from incorrect perceptions, or the incorrect processing of information by the consumer, were discussed in Chapter 5. However, we said little about the process of deliberation itself and other elements of the buying process. (See Figure 10.) This chapter deals with

Deliberation and evaluation

Preference and choice

Buying intentions

Post-purchase satisfaction

DELIBERATION AND EVALUATION

There are three buying situations that involve no meaningful deliberation either to appraise a product or to evaluate rival brands:

1. *Habit,* where the consumer implicitly follows the rule of buying the same brand as before.
2. *Picking,* where consumer choice is either made at random or based on mere whim.
3. *Intrinsic preference,* where brand choice is a matter of what the consumer likes at the time.

In each of these situations, which were discussed in detail in Chapter 4, brand choice is not the result of conscious deliberation, although there may have been deliberation in the past leading the consumer to adopt the policy of making brand choice a matter of habit or picking.

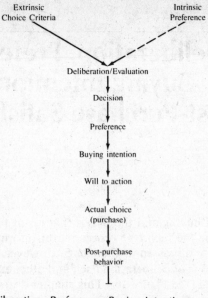

Figure 10 Deliberation, Preference, Buying Intentions, and Post-Purchase Behavior

Whenever the consumer takes account of both use and generated functions, we have assumed that deliberation occurs to resolve tradeoffs and uncertainties. However, on occasion, the consumer may use just a single criterion, such as convention, in which case no meaningful prepurchase deliberation will occur. A more ambiguous situation occurs when the consumer has no option as to brand because of monopolistic conditions or the temporary unavailability of alternatives. In such a situation, the consumer who is buying for the first time might deliberate about whether it is preferable to buy or forego the product altogether.

With habit, picking, or intrinsic preference, the consumer either sees choice as unproblematic or believes that the remaining factual uncertainties are not worth bothering about. There may be other situations, such as those charged with emotion, where conscious deliberation is bypassed. It may also be that the reasons given for the occasional purchase of certain trivial or low-involvement products could result from consumers' observing their own buying actions and then deducing justifying reasons. Some of these justifying reasons might be the same as those given in advertisements for the product. It was to avoid such post-purchase rationalizations that it was recommended that protocol statements cover anticipatory and contemporaneous accounts and not just retrospective ones.

The Compensatory Decision Strategy

Where deliberation to resolve uncertainty does occur, choice is the result of a decision-making process. This process is usually assumed to follow some sequence. We have assumed that the consumer's choice criteria express goals, wants, and beliefs while the relative importance attached to the various categories of choice criteria reflect the consumer's value system. *But by what "decision strategy" does the consumer move from choice criteria to brand choice?* Does the consumer act as if he or she weights the individual attributes for relative importance and then combines the results in some simple additive way to arrive at an overall evaluation of one brand vis-à-vis another? This is the assumption of the compensatory model. It is termed a *compensatory model* because the consumer accepts that a product's weaknesses in one respect can be compensated by strength in another.

It is assumed that the relative worth of an offering to the consumer is simply arrived at by taking the sum of the assessed values of the individual brand attributes. On this assumption, the whole is simply the sum of the individual parts, and each attribute is assumed to make an independent contribution to the overall worth of the offering; interactive effects are ignored. There are, however, nonlinear, noncompensatory models that may be better suited to certain buying decisions (Einhorn, 1970).

The Non-Compensatory Decision Strategy

While a compensatory decision strategy assumes the consumer makes tradeoffs, a noncompensatory decision strategy makes no such assumption that a brand's weakness in one attribute can be compensated by strengths in another. Thus, under the "conjunctive rule," the consumer eliminates from consideration all those brands that fall below some minimum level: any brand falling below the cut-off point on the attribute dimension of interest is rejected. In this way, brands are divided into those that are acceptable and those that are not acceptable. Under the

"disjunctive rule" the consumer demands some attribute be
above some minimum level: those brands that do not possess
such an attribute are regarded as unacceptable. The operation of
the conjunctive and disjunctive rules is often implicit in protocol statements, for example, "I will not consider a car that seats
less than four people" (conjunctive rule) and "I want a car that
has either sufficient gas mileage or sufficient acceleration" (disjunctive rule).

Another decision strategy is the "lexiographic rule." It
assumes that alternative offerings are first compared on the most
important attribute first. The brand that is "in a class of its own"
on this attribute is the one selected. If several brands are equally
good on the attribute, selection depends on which brand performs best on the next most important attribute, and so on.
Under the lexiographic rule, the consumer arrives at a unique
choice instead of merely eliminating the unacceptable.

Compensatory Versus Non-Compensatory Strategies

There is a good deal of research on the use of compensatory versus noncompensatory strategies. Thus, one study showed that
when the number of alternatives to be evaluated was small, subjects used a compensatory decision strategy. When the number
of alternatives increased, subjects used a noncompensatory
(conjunctive) strategy to evaluate the remainder (Lussier and
Olshavsky, 1979). Another study showed that subjects faced
with a choice between just two options searched for the same
amount of information on each alternative in a way consistent
with applying a compensatory strategy. However, with a large
number of alternatives from which to choose (6–12 alternatives), the search for information across the various alternatives
varied in a way that suggested the use of a noncompensatory
strategy to first reduce the number of alternatives to a manageable number (Payne, 1976).

It may be, as one study suggests, that once the number of alternatives is reduced to a manageable number by the use of the
conjunctive and/or disjunctive rule, the choice process tends to
involve evaluating pairs of alternatives and not individual evaluations (Russo and Rosen, 1975). Even when alternatives are
not directly compatible (e.g., deciding between a TV set and a
refrigerator), it may still be that a choice is made between them
from a consideration of the value of the individual attributes of

each option: combining attribute values or utilities into some overall score as a basis for choice (Johnson, 1984).

Other aspects of information processing are also a topic of much current research. One study shows the importance of presentation (Bettman and Kakkar, 1977). The results of this study were in line with the so-called principle of "concreteness" to the effect that a decision-maker tends only to use that information that is explicitly displayed and will process it only in the form in which it is displayed, so that what has to be inferred, stored, or transformed in some way tends to be discounted or ignored.

Another study found that consumers with a moderate amount of knowledge and experience with a product did more processing of the available information than did consumers with high or low amounts of knowledge and experience with a product. In addition, attribute evaluation tended to occur in the early stages of buying and brand evaluation later on in the process (Bettman and Park, 1980). (This is also a common finding in protocol statements.)

Of course, the consumer may on occasion rank rival brands on the basis of just overall impression, without paying much attention to any specific attribute.

The Process of Decision-Making

In this book, we have assumed the choice criteria of consumers in decision-making are an expression of goals, wants, and weighting of the various choice criteria. The choice criteria are viewed as emanating from the consumer's system of values. Left unqualified, this view of the process is somewhat simplistic in that it assumes a set sequence and fails to recognize the conceptual and process interdependencies between the different elements of decision-making.

The goals of preferred life vision of the consumer typically *underdetermine* (i.e., do not completely determine) wants. Although it is agreed that people do have an acute sense of their own self-interest and that this manifests itself in whatever they do, it is also true that each of the consumer's higher level goals could find expression in any number of product wants. Two consumers with the same higher level goals or preferred life vision need not have the same product wants.

As a consequence of having life goals, consumers express these goals in their wants. These wants are subsequently shaped into choice criteria by beliefs about both individual circumstances and the available offerings. Choice criteria are developed to different degrees of specificity depending on circumstances, availability of information, and the extent to which consumers resolve conflicting demands within themselves. Technical and legalistic criteria in particular are likely to be specific to circumstances, while integrative criteria are perhaps more affected by personality and the socialization process. (See Figure 11.) In any case, the consumer's choice criteria may not be definite and can often be vague.

Even where the consumer's choice criteria become sufficiently developed for the consumer to state a definite product preference, the choice criteria may still not be specific enough to determine brand preference (e.g., where picking occurs). Even where choice criteria are sufficient to determine brand preference, they are often open to revision. This is because it is difficult to demonstrate that the choice criteria (including the relative importance of criteria) adopted are the best since such criteria are likely to be the result of many uneasy compromises by the consumer.

Choice criteria, as initially developed, are often inadequate for selecting the one best brand because they may not be sufficient to determine a comparative preference. Where choice criteria are so broad that any brand will do, picking behavior is the result.

If life goals are underdetermining of wants, and wants are underdetermining of choice criteria, and choice criteria are themselves open to certain revision, it can be misleading for a marketing manager to simply assume wants are fixed. The extent to which consumers act with a clear idea of their wants can easily be exaggerated. It can be even more misleading when manufacturers interpret consumer wants not only as fixed but as being concerned only with use functions: meeting perceived use functions better than the competition may not be enough to attract customers.

The Tradeoff Process

Consumers act for reasons, but such reasons need not meet the standard of "good" reasons as defined by others. Ideally, the consumer seeks to meet certain technical, legalistic, integrative, adaptive, and intrinsic choice criteria with the minimum eco-

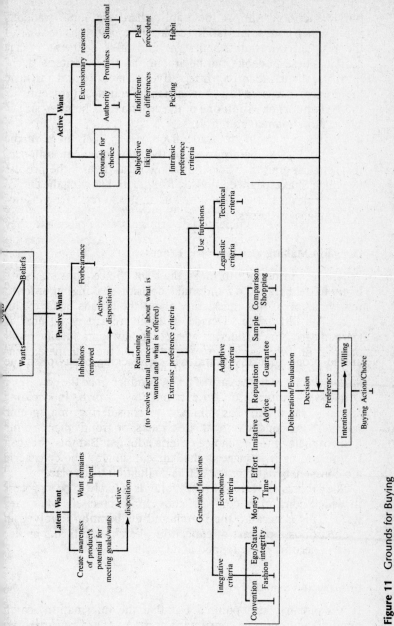

Figure 11 Grounds for Buying

nomic sacrifice. Almost inevitably, there are some tradeoffs about which consumers fail to reach firm conclusions because of the residual uncertainties that remain after deliberation has ceased. These tradeoffs can be among the choice criteria (technical, legalistic, adaptive, integrative, economic, and intrinsic preference) discussed (e.g., between more rainwear protection or more glamour) or within one of the criteria (e.g., between size of car or more maneuverability).

Finding out about the tradeoff process is likely to never be complete. Just as merely knowing the rules of seventeenth-century English grammar does not allow us to deduce the process by which Shakespeare composed *King Lear,* knowing the choice criteria rules is not enough to tell us all the secrets of a consumer's thought processes.

Decision-Making as a Learning Process

Where it is important to make the right choice, consumers are likely to deliberate (i.e., undertake decision-making) in order to resolve some of the uncertainty about the brands being evaluated. The old adage "Decide in haste, repent at leisure" is learned early. In considering whether to buy some specific product, the consumer decides on whether or not the anticipated benefits of possession are sufficient to outweigh the costs. This is not an easy decision in the case of a new product since the consumer is assessing future promise and unknown worth. In deciding among rival brands (as opposed to considering one specific product), the consumer evaluates, ranks, or groups them on the basis of their fit to the choice criteria adopted. But this, too, can be misleading if it suggests that the consumer's choice criteria are completely determined before evaluation takes place.

The process of evaluating rival brands is likely to be a process in which consumers come to know more precisely what they want. This is because the search and deliberation involved in evaluation is a process of education whereby wants and choice criteria become more refined and specific.

Information Search

It has already been pointed out that the information search undertaken to resolve consumer uncertainty need be carried no further than that required to establish a preference. There are pressures to minimize the information search (e.g., time pressure, the sacrifice of postponing gratification, and the way money can burn a hole in the pocket until a choice is made). An extensive formal search for relevant product information does occur on occasion. But much information is perhaps acquired casually, by a wide-awake interest in the social scene.

Dissatisfied Buyers

If the realities of the market oblige consumers to make purchases that fail to meet part of their choice criteria or fall below what might reasonably be expected, consumers may still continue to buy rather than forego the product. However, they will remain dissatisfied. Many products, such as hair restorers, weight reducers, and anti-perspirants, fall below what might reasonably be expected. As a consequence, newcomers to the market find it easy to get consumers to try the brand—but unless the new brand has that extra something, trial does not lead to repeat sales.

PREFERENCE AND CHOICE

The word "choice" has several different meanings. In the study of ethics, choice is often used to refer to the mental act of volition in deciding between alternatives—in which case choice is part of the decision-making process. As such, it is often contrasted with "preference" which may occur spontaneously and divorced from any decision process. "Choice" is also used as a synonym for the decision resulting from the decision process. Another definition conceptualizes "choice" as the mental act of selection that always precedes action. (However, it has yet to be demonstrated that such mental acts do always occur prior to action.) In research on buyer behavior, "Choice" is defined in yet another way—namely, as the overt physical act of taking or getting one object from a range of alternatives. If choice is an overt physical action, then preference precedes it. In other words, preference results *in* choice rather than *from* choice. Here, as is the practice in marketing, we will follow the latter viewpoint. From our point of view, this is more useful.

The Concept of Preference

For consumers to prefer brand A to brand B means consumers desire that they have brand "A" and not brand "B" (Schick,

1984). Hence preferences are likely to be predictive of what brands are bought if buying actually does occur. However, asking consumers about their preferences is not free of problems:

- Is it intrinsic or extrinsic preference that is of interest? If asked "Which car do you prefer?" the consumer might point to a sports car that coincides with his or her liking (or *in*trinsic preference), but if asked "Which car would you prefer if you were buying," the consumer's extrinsic preference might lead to a different response.

- Expressed preferences of consumers cannot just be considered independent of the buying situation. On the one hand, expressed preferences may be just sour grapes (Elster, 1983) in that consumers may reject, as their preference, that which is beyond their reach even though it is what they secretly prefer. On the other hand, it is not unknown for consumers to state they prefer the unusual just to be different.

- Preferences are not absolute. They vary over time and with the occasion. Hence, it must be decided whether interest in consumer preferences centers on asking consumers what they *always* prefer, what they *usually* prefer, or what they prefer on *this occasion*.

- Expressed preferences may change when the consumer is provided with further information. Many preferences are based on inadequate information and even false beliefs.

- If the consumer's first preference is unavailable, it does not follow that the second preference will be bought. The consumer might instead prefer an entirely different product. For example, if Dannon yogurt was the consumer's first preference and the X brand of yogurt was the second preference, it might well be that the consumer prefers Baskin-Robbins' ice cream to all other yogurts but Dannon (although he prefers Dannon yogurt to ice cream). Thus, the net preference for Dannon yogurt is not the utility or satisfaction of consuming this brand against the sacrifice of the second preference brand of yogurt but the utility or satisfaction of consuming Dannon yogurt against the sacrifice of Baskin-Robbins' ice cream. (Schick, 1984.)

Choice Criteria and Preference

Consumers with the same choice criteria do not necessarily prefer the same brand: they might have different beliefs as to which brand best embodies their choice criteria. The consumer infers the degree to which the rival brands match the buying rules or choice criteria. It is this process that leads to different beliefs about the relative desirability of rival brands. Hence, knowledge of the signs and observations consumers use to make inferences about the characteristics of the offering, and judgments about the extent to which each rival offering meets the choice criteria is essential. Differences in inference processes may explain why two rival brands can have radically different sales yet be identical in product attributes, distribution, and price. The more successful firm may have been better able to match their brand to the consumer's choice criteria in their promotions. (A rival hypothesis might be that the less successful brand is a late market entry providing no reason to switch brands.)

Choice and Preference

If choice is regarded as an overt action, then the choices consumers actually make can be used as an operational measure of preferences. However, choices are not always in line with expressed preferences for the reasons already given or because of situational factors or because of a last minute change of mind. In any case, choices need not be based on a decision: with habitual choices, choice is based on past precedent; with picking, choice is based on whim or some random process. The fact that people are creatures of habit facilitates the prediction of behavior. Much of everyday buying is done in accordance with well-formed habits. As far as day-to-day buying is concerned, consumers may be on "automatic pilot," only stopping to deliberate when difficulties or perceived opportunities arise.

Consumer purchase does not merely reveal or expose what the consumer's choice was all along. The purchase that follows a decision may be something very different from the consumer's initial inclinations.

BUYING INTENTIONS

Intentions can be contrasted with wants (Meiland, 1970). The consumer can want to buy something without actually intending to do so. Consumers can knowingly have wants that conflict (e.g., to remain slim yet to eat whatever one likes) but can never knowingly have conflicting intentions (e.g., to intend to buy yet to intend not to buy). Finally, wants are satisfied while intentions are carried out. If the satisfaction of wants is the purpose of buying, beliefs specify expression of the want while buying intentions provide the resolve to take some action toward buying.

Consumers may believe they need a particular product and, within that product class, have a brand preference. Nonetheless, they may not move on to the next stage in buying as wants and beliefs may not always be sufficient to bring about a conscious buying intention. A conscious buying intention is a disposition, amounting to some resolve, to buy some particular product or brand *under certain specified circumstances.* For example, when a consumer announces the intention to buy a Mercedes next week, that intention might really mean:

- The purchase will only be made if the consumer wins the lottery, so the intention is conditional.
- The consumer believes it is not probable he will buy a Mercedes next week because he realizes it is highly improbable he will win the lottery on which the buying of the Mercedes depends.
- The consumer has not considered what is involved in buying a Mercedes, and, after such consideration, may change his mind.

An intention to buy something is not the same as an unconditional, categorical prediction of a purchase. When the consumer says, "I *will* buy a Mercedes tomorrow at Alford's" and is using "I will" in the sense of a prediction, it is different than saying "I *intend* to buy a Mercedes tomorrow at Alford's" (Meiland, 1970; B. O'Shaughnessy, 1980).

"I *will . . .* " is a prediction that is made true by a subsequent action. "I *intend . . .* " is only made true by the presence of a state of mind and reports of the existence of that state. A prediction is falsified when it does not happen, but an intention is not. In other words, a consumer who says "I intend to buy a Mercedes car next week at Alford's" is really saying "If the situation now were just like the situation I visualize [or fantasize!] next week, I would buy a Mercedes now." Buying intentions always refer to a state of mind and are always conditional in terms of time, place, and circumstances. Hence, in inquiring about consumer intentions, we should focus on confirming the existence of the intention state and the resolve and assumptions that lie behind it.

Intention and Voluntary Action

The question arises as to whether all voluntary purchases are preceded by an intention to buy. If by the term "intention" we mean a resolve emanating from *conscious* deliberation, then an intention need not precede buying. In day-to-day shopping, many items are bought as a result of just seeing them. If buyers were questioned, they would acknowledge they had no intention of buying the product before entering the store. In other words, they never *planned* to buy the product. However, this is not the same as saying they never intended to buy the product (even at the time of purchase), for this would be to acknowledge having made an error (e.g., mistaking the item for something else).

The voluntary act of buying presupposes an intent—though not necessarily a conscious intent—to buy. Every voluntary act based on a reason is an intentional act.

Intentions in Preferences

Where buying intentions appear out of line with preferences, consumers seem inconsistent since what they intend to do contradicts their prior judgment. There can be a last minute change of mind, however, as when new information is received or when the consumer gives way to a desire for instant gratification not in line with long-term interests. Whenever emotion takes a hand (e.g., through strong positive or negative evaluations of something associated with the product) there is less attention to long-term interests. Attention is channeled onto more limited choice criteria and cues than would normally be the case. Pears (1984) speaks of strong desires having a way of achieving gratification without having to pass through the checkpoint of an evaluation (decision) process and of reason having to work, so to speak, by persuasion rather than command.

Knowing and Intending

A conscious intention to buy brand X is a resolve and a plan to buy it. But for a consumer to *know* she is going to buy X is not the same as consciously *intending* to buy X since a conscious intention is a *personal* commitment to buy at some time and place given certain circumstances. Thus, I may know that I'll be buying candy for the children next week although it is not my conscious intention to do so. Sellers must fall in line with the time/place dimension of the buyer's plan (e.g., on delivery/availability). Otherwise the seller is in effect asking buyers to alter their intentions. This explains why stock must be on hand when consumers are ready to buy. For example, a consumer who plans to buy a bed is not likely to postpone buying for months while waiting for the preferred model to arrive.

Intention and Will

A consumer may form an intention to buy a particular product and may even take appropriate intentional movements toward buying and yet never actually buy because of a change of mind; the forgetting of the intention; or being prevented from carrying out the intention (perhaps through the nonavailability of the product). Initial intentions often change in the process of shopping, so we should not expect a high correlation between these initial intentions and actual purchases.

In particular, intentions as to what brand to buy are apt to change because shopping is an educational process that leads to new beliefs about what is available and about the relative merits of rival brands. Moreover, the presence of a buying intention is not always a sufficient resolve to buy. It may be that forming an intention to buy is analogous to simply "putting an active faculty into gear" and that there is still a need to *will* the event before the consumer takes the final step of "depressing the accelerator" to actually buy (McGinn, 1983). We are all familiar with people going through the motions of (say) buying a house as if following an intention to buy and yet never quite bringing themselves (i.e., conjuring up the will) to finally complete the transaction. We recognize that not all intentions are firm but are sometimes half-hearted. In general, intentions to buy that are endorsed by the consumer as consistent with long-term best interests and which in other ways can be carried out wholeheartedly without reservations are the ones more likely to remain firm.

Triggering Buying

A want supplies the motivating force to stimulate interest; belief provides this force with reasons for favoring some specific product or brand; intention prepares the consumer to undertake buying action; and will puts the purchase plan into action. The fact that wants and beliefs favoring buying are not in themselves always sufficient to bring about buying intention, nor is the intention to buy necessarily sufficient to ensure buying action, highlights the need for triggering mechanisms (such as sales promotions) to move the buyer from a disposition to buy, to a buying intention, and, finally, to the *will* to make a choice.

POST-PURCHASE SATISFACTION

After buying a product the consumer may be:

Completely satisfied with the product.
Satisfied with the product as a whole but dissatisfied with some aspect of it.
Dissatisfied with the product.

A consumer does not necessarily cease to buy a certain product or brand simply because of dissatisfaction with the product. Consumers may know before they purchase that they will be dissatisfied—but they buy nonetheless because they believe the brand is better than rival brands and they are not prepared to do without. Customer satisfaction is not a necessary condition for the consumer to go on buying a product. Many products considered unsatisfactory are still purchased because of the absence of better substitutes. If consumers consider the function for which the product is bought to be essential, they will continue to buy even if the product falls below expectations until something better comes along. Consumers abandon a product or brand when the accumulation of dissatisfactions is perceived to be more than those of the substitute rival brand. Consumers do not necessarily switch because their own brand does not measure up to some reasonable standard.

Not all goods are "search goods" (e.g., a tie) about which we can learn from shopping. Many goods are "experience goods" (e.g., personal computers) that must be learned about through experience. The consumer's evaluation of such experience may not always be the most rational, but if unfavorable, it may lead consumers to "bad-mouth" a brand. Hence the importance of trying to settle grievances to the customer's satisfaction.

Some product dissatisfaction may arise because the product or brand did not live up to an advertised promise. However, some customers may be dissatisfied with a purchase even if it turns out to be *exactly* what they had in mind. Satisfying the customer's want at the time of purchase does not necessarily ensure post-purchase satisfaction. Wants can be met without the satisfaction anticipated—as frequently happens with children's toys.

Post-purchase experience with a product bought for the first time is always a learning experience in which consumers themselves may come to know better what they want. They may find that what they now want is not what they wanted at the time of purchase. For example, a telephone answering machine that only allows for a 20-second message may prove to be insufficient for the consumer.

Even if the customer is satisfied after purchasing, consuming, or using the brand, this does not guarantee that the same brand will be bought next time around. What is bought on any one occasion is very much dependent on what is available at the time; more attractive offerings may have become available in the meantime.

Customer satisfaction does not even guarantee that the functions for which the product is bought are being met. The consumer may not be able to directly establish the presence of some attribute (e.g., the wearability of a carpet) but infers the attribute from surrogate indicators (e.g., the carpet was used on the floor of a well-trafficked store). In addition, evaluating the performance of functions may not be straightforward. Consumers can and do err in evaluating their experience with a brand. Experience itself can be ambiguous. Hence, the use of a placebo when experimenting with new medicines. In any case, it is sometimes other people's opinion that counts, not personal experience. Thus, I may continue to use a hair preparation because my friends think it improves my appearance, even though I cannot see a difference.

SUMMARY

The consumer's choice criteria may be sufficiently developed to know what product is wanted but not sufficiently developed to determine brand preference. Choice criteria are often open to revision as they are apt to result from many uneasy compromises by the consumer. If choice criteria are open to persuasion, it is misleading to take the consumer's want as fixed and given. It is even more misleading to assume the consumer's major interest always lies in core use functions and economy functions. Asking consumers about their preferences must take into account:

1. The possibility of conflict between intrinsic and extrinsic preference.

2. The possibility of consumers rejecting as their preference what they believe to be out of reach (the sour grapes phenomenon) or alternatively accepting as their preference the glamour of the unknown (the grass always being greener on the other side of the fence phenomenon).

3. The possibility of preferences varying with the occasion or over time.

4. The possibility of preferences being changed by further information.

5. The possibility of the consumer being only interested in the brand preferred so that the nonavailability of that brand does not lead to the buying of a rival brand.

Consumers with seemingly the same choice criteria can prefer different brands if they use different rules to infer the degree to which the choice criteria are present or absent. Firms with the largest market share may, on occasion, only differ from rivals in successfully signalling the match between their brand's characteristics and the signs used by the consumer to check that the brand possesses what is sought.

Wants and beliefs may lead to brand preference, but may be insufficiently firm to lead to buying intention. A buying intention ("I intend to buy") should be distinguished from a prediction ("I will buy"). Buying intentions always refer to a state of mind and are always conditional in terms of time, place, and circumstances. Intentions that are consistent with long-term interests and can be carried out wholeheartedly are the ones most likely to be firm and followed by the *will* to buy.

Consumers may be dissatisfied with a brand but continue to buy it because they believe rival brands are no better and are not prepared to do without the product. Consumers can be dissatisfied with a purchase even when it turns out to be exactly what they had in mind at the time of purchase. Benefits do not always come up to expectations in terms of satisfaction yielded.

Consumers may be satisfied with a brand but fail to buy the brand next time around. This may occur because rival offerings have become more attractive. Consumers may be satisfied with a product or brand even though it fails to meet the functions for which it was bought. This happens when consumers use the wrong signs to infer the desired effects.

Implications for Marketing

1. If consumers choose the firm's product as a result of a decision process, the firm should seek to influence the consumer's choice criteria right up to the point of sale since such criteria are likely to remain open to persuasion throughout the stages of buying.

2. A firm should not just assume the consumer's want is fixed and given, but should consider influencing the buying decision by trying to change consumer choice criteria by changing perceptions.

3. The firm should not seek to provide information on everything there is to know about a product but only information that is sufficient to establish brand preference and demonstrate their brand's superiority.

4. A firm should ensure that it is providing the same signals as consumers use to infer the presence of their choice criteria.

5. If buying intentions are to lead to buying, the firm should consider ways (triggering mechanisms) by which intentions to buy the firm's product are translated into a *will* to buy.

6. A firm should not just rest content with knowing its sales are at the right level, but should research customer satisfaction with its brand since
   (a) Consumers may be dissatisfied with a brand when it fails to meet reasonable expectations and so are disposed to switch to competitive offerings when those are made available.
   (b) The benefits realized might come up to consumer expectations but the yield in terms of post-purchase satisfaction may not be as anticipated.

7. A firm should check whether new competitive offerings are being perceived as a better buy since current customer satisfaction is always conditional on rival offerings being less attractive.

References

Adler, Mortimer J. (1985). *Ten Philosophical Mistakes.* New York: Macmillan.

Ajzen, I., and Fishbein, M. (1980). *Understanding Attitudes and Predicting Social Behavior.* N.J.: Prentice-Hall.

Anderson, John R. (1983). *The Architecture of Cognition.* Cambridge, Mass.: Harvard University Press.

Beck, Lewis White (1975). *The Actor and the Spectator.* New Haven, Conn.: Yale University Press.

Becker, Gary Stanley (1976). *The Economic Approach to Human Behavior.* Chicago: University of Chicago Press.

Bell, David E. (1982). "Regret in Decision Making under Uncertainty," *Operations Research,* Vol 30, No. 5 (September–October): 961–981.

Bell, David E. (1985). "Disappointment in Decision Making under Uncertainty," *Operations Research,* Vol. 33, No. 1 (January–February): 2–27.

Bettman, James, and Kakkar, Pradeep (1977). "Effects of Information Presentation Format on Consumer Information Acquisition Strategies," *Journal of Consumer Research,* Vol. 3 (March): 233–240.

Bettman, James R., and Park, C. Whan (1980). "Effects of Prior Knowledge and Experience and Phase of the Choice Process on Consumer Decision Processes: A Protocol Analysis," *Journal of Consumer Research,* Vol. 7 (December): 234–248.

Black, Max (1970). *Margins of Precision.* Ithaca, N.Y.: Cornell University Press.

Bourne, Francis S. (1957). "Group Influence in Marketing and Public Relations" in *Some Applications of Behavioral Research,* ed. Rensis Likert and Samuel P. Hayes. Paris: UNESCO.

Calhoun, Cheshire (1984). "Cognitive Emotions?" in *What Is an Emo-*

tion? ed. Cheshire Calhoun and Robert C. Solomon. New York: Oxford University Press.

Culver, C. M., and Gert, B. (1982). *Philosophy in Medicine.* New York: Oxford University Press.

Diesing, Paul (1962). *Reason in Society: Five Types of Decisions and Their Social Conditions.* Urbana, Ill.: University of Illinois Press.

Dilman, Ilham (1981). *Studies in Language and Reason.* Totowa, N.J.: Barnes and Noble.

Douglas, Mary (and Isherwood, B.) (1979). *The World of Goods.* New York: Basic Books.

Einhorn, Hillel (1970). "The Use of Nonlinear, Noncompensatory Models in Decision Making," *Psychological Bulletin,* Vol. 73, No. 3: 221–230.

Elster, Jon (1983). *Sour Grapes: Studies in the Subversion of Rationality.* Cambridge, Mass.: Cambridge University Press.

Ericsson, K., Anders, and Simon, Herbert A. (1980). "Verbal Reports as Data," *Psychological Review,* Vol. 87, No. 3 (May): 215–251.

Foxall, Gordon R. (1975). "Social Factors in Consumer Choice: Replication and Extension," *Journal of Consumer Research,* Vol. 2 (June): 60–64.

Garfinkel, H. (1967). *Studies in Ethnomethodology.* Englewood Cliffs, N.J.: Prentice-Hall.

Gay, Peter (1985). *Freud for Historians.* New York: Oxford University Press.

Goffman, E. (1963). *Stigma: Notes on the Management of Spoiled Identity.* Englewood Cliffs, N.J.: Prentice-Hall.

Gosling, J. C. B. (1969). *Pleasure and Desire: The Case for Hedonism Reviewed.* Oxford: Clarendon Press.

Harman, Gilbert (1973). *Thought.* Princeton, N.J.: Princeton University Press.

Harré, R., and Secord, P. F. (1973). *The Explanation of Social Behavior.* Littlefield, N.J.: Adams & Co.

Hogarth, Robin M., and Makridakis, Spyros (1981). "Forecasting and Planning: An Evaluation," *Management Science,* Vol. 27, No. 2 (February): 115–138.

Humphrey, N. (1983). *Consciousness Regained.* New York: Oxford University Press.

Jacoby, J., Chestnut, R. W., and Fisher, W. A. (1978). "A Behavioral Process Approach to Information Acquisition in Nondurable Purchasing," *Journal of Marketing Research,* Vol. 15 (November): 532–544.

Johnson, Michael D. (1984). "Consumer Choice Strategies for Comparing Noncomparable Alternatives," *Journal of Consumer Research,* Vol. 11 (December): 741–753.

Kahneman, Daniel, Slovic, Paul, and Tversky, Amos (1982). *Judgement under Uncertainty: Heuristics and Biases.* New York: Cambridge University Press.

Kahneman, Daniel, and Tversky, Amos (1984). "Choices, Values, and Frames," *American Psychologist,* Vol. 39, No. 4: 341–350.

Kahneman, D., and Tversky, A. (1982). "The Psychology of Preferences." *Scientific American,* Vol. 246, No. 1 (January): 160–173.

Katona, George, and Mueller, Eva (1954). "A Study of Purchase Decisions" in *Consumer Behavior: The Dynamics of Consumer Reaction,* ed. Lincoln H. Clark. New York: New York University Press.

Kirsh, David (1983). "The Role of Philosophy in the Human Sciences" in *The Need for Interpretation,* eds. Sollace Mitchell and Michael Rosen. New York: Humanities Press.

Knox, M. (1968). *Action.* Boston: George Allen and Unwin.

Krantz, David (1967). "Rational Distance Functions for Multidimensional Scaling," *Journal of Mathematical Psychology,* Vol. 4: 226–245.

Kron, Joan (1983). "The Status Merchants," *New York,* September 5, 1983.

Langford, Glenn (1971). *Human Action.* New York: Doubleday & Co.

Laudan, Larry (1984). *Science and Values.* Berkeley, Calif.: University of California Press.

Levi, Isaac (1985). "Illusions about Uncertainty," *British Journal of Philosophy of Science,* Vol. 36: 331–340.

Lewis, David K. (1969). *Conventions: A Philosophical Study.* Cambridge, Mass.: Harvard University Press.

Leymore, V. L. (1975). *The Hidden Myth.* New York: Basic Books.

Locander, W. B., and Hermann, P. W. (1979). "The Effect of Self-Confidence and Anxiety on Information Seeking in Consumer Risk Reduction," *Journal of Marketing Research,* Vol. 16 (May): 268–274.

Lurie, Alison (1983). *The Language of Clothes.* New York: Vintage Books.

Lussier, Denis A., and Olshavsky, Richard W. (1979). "Task Complexity and Contingent Processing in Brand Choice," *Journal of Consumer Research,* Vol. 6 (September): 154–165.

MacIntyre, Alasdair (1971). "The Idea of a Social Science" in *Rationality,* ed. Bryan R. Wilson. New York: Harper Torchbook.

March, James G. (1978). "Bounded Rationality, Ambiguity, and the Engineering of Choice," *The Bell Journal of Economics,* Vol. 9: 587–608.

Marchand, Roland (1985). *Advertising the American Dream.* Berkeley, Calif.: University of California Press.

McGinn, C. (1983). *The Character of Mind.* New York: Oxford University Press.

McGrath, N. W. (1983). *Top Sellers U.S.A.* New York: William Morrow & Co.

Meiland, Jack W. (1970). *The Nature of Intention.* London: Methuen & Co.

Moschis, George P. (1976). "Social Comparisons and Informal Group Influences," *Journal of Marketing Research,* Vol. 13 (August): 237–244.

Newman, Joseph W., and Staelin, Richard (1973). "Information Sources of Durable Goods," *Journal of Advertising Research,* Vol. 13, No. 2 (April): 19–29.

Nisbett, R. E., and Wilson, T. D. (1977). "Telling More Than We Know: Verbal Reports and Mental Processes," *Psychological Review,* Vol. 84: 231–259.

Nolt, J. E. (1984). *Informal Logic: Possible Worlds and Imagination.* New York: McGraw-Hill.

Nozick, Robert (1981). *Philosophical Explanations.* Boston, Mass.: The Belknap Press, Harvard University.

O'Shaughnessy, B. (1980). *The Will: A Dual Aspect Theory.* Cambridge, Mass.: Cambridge University Press.

Payne, John W. (1976). "Task Complexity and Contingent Processing in Decision Making: An Information Search and Protocol Analysis," *Organizational Behavior and Human Performance,* Vol. 16 (August): 366–387.

Pears, David (1984). *Motivated Irrationality.* Oxford: Clarendon Press.

Peters, R. S. (1958). *The Concept of Motivation.* London: Routledge and Kegan Paul.

Poffenberger, Albert Theodore (1925). *Psychology in Advertising.* Chicago: A. W. Shaw Company.

Putnam, Hilary (1981). *Reason, Truth and History.* Cambridge, Mass.: Cambridge University Press.

Raz, Joseph (1975). *Practical Reason and Norms.* London: Hutchinson University Library.

Robertson, T. S. (1976). "Low Commitment Consumer Behavior," *Journal of Advertising Research,* Vol. 16 (April): 19–24.

Roselius, Ted (1971). "Consumer Rankings of Risk Reduction Methods," *Journal of Marketing,* Vol. 35, No. 1 (January): 56–61.

Russo, J. Edward, and Rosen, Larry D. (1975). "An Eye Fixation Analysis of Multialternative Choice," *Memory and Cognition,* Vol. 3, No. 3: (May): 267–276.

Ryan, Alan (1978). "Maximizing, Moralising and Dramatising" in *Action and Interpretation,* eds. Christopher Hookway and Phillip Pettit. Cambridge, Mass.: Cambridge University Press.

Rychlak, Joseph F. (1979). *Discovering Free Will.* New York: Oxford University Press.

Schick, F. (1984). *Having Reasons: An Essay on Rationality and Sociality.* Princeton, N.J.: Princeton University Press.

Shaper, Eva (1983). *Pleasure, Preference and Value.* Cambridge, Mass.: Cambridge University Press.

Sheth, Jagdish, N. (1968). "How Adults Learn Brand Preference," *Journal of Advertising Research,* Vol. 8 (September): 25–36.

Shwayder, D. (1965). *The Stratification of Behavior.* New York: The Humanities Press.

Smith, E. R., and Miller, F. D. (1978). "Limits on Perception of Cognitive Processes: A Reply to Nisbett and Wilson," *Psychological Review,* Vol. 85, No. 4: 355–362.

Solomon, R. C. (1980). "Emotions and Choice" in *Explaining Emotion,* ed. Amelie Oksenberg Rorty. Berkeley, Calif.: University of California Press.

Solomon, R. C. (1984). "Emotions and Choice" in *What Is an Emotion?* ed. Cheshire Calhoun and Robert C. Solomon. New York: Oxford University Press.

Taylor, Charles (1964). *The Explanation of Behavior.* London: Routledge and Kegan Paul.

Taylor, Charles (1979). "Action as Expression" in *Intention and Intentionality,* ed. Cora Diamond and Jenny Teichman. Ithaca, N.Y.: Cornell University Press.

Taylor, Richard (1966). *Action and Purpose.* Englewood Cliffs, N.J.: Prentice-Hall.

Ullman-Margalit, E., and Morgenbesser, S. (1977). "Picking and Choosing," *Social Research,* Vol. 44 (Winter): 757–785.

Venkatesan, M. (1966). "Experimental Study of Consumer Behavior Conformity and Independence," *Journal of Marketing Research,* Vol. 3 (November): 384–387.

Von Wright, G. H. (1962). *The Logic of Preference.* Edinburgh: Edinburgh University Press.

Von Wright, G. H. (1971). *Explanation and Understanding.* Ithaca, N.Y.: Cornell University Press.

Von Wright, G. H. (1983). *Practical Reason.* Oxford: Basil Blackwood.

Webster, M. (1975). *Actions and Actors.* Cambridge, Mass.: Winthrop Publishers Inc.

Winch, P. G. (1958). *The Idea of a Social Science.* London: Routledge and Kegan Paul.

Zajonc, Robert, and Markus, Hazel (1982). "Affective and Cognitive Factors in Preferences," *Journal of Consumer Research,* Vol. 9 (September): 123–131.

Index